Matthew Glendinning was born in Southampton in 1962. He is a freelance sportswriter and broadcaster. He lives in North London.

Victoria Glendinning is an award-winning biographer of Trollope, Elizabeth Bowen, Vita Sackville-West, Edith Sitwell, Rebecca West and of her great-Aunt, Winnie Seebohm (*A Suppressed Cry*). She is also a literary critic, broadcaster, writer on travel and gardening and author of two novels, *The Grown Ups* and *Electricity*. She lives in London.

Sons & Mothers

Edited by
MATTHEW GLENDINNING
and
VICTORIA GLENDINNING

C o n t e n t s

Introduction

When we decided to undertake this book, at the suggestion of Lennie Goodings at Virago, we were both agreed on one thing. We knew what we *didn't* want *Sons and Mothers* to be. We didn't want it to be cosy, or bland, or written from one particular social or ideological standpoint. We didn't want it to be a coffee-table forgettable. The more we talked about what we didn't want, the clearer became the image of the living book that it might turn out to be.

The subject, even at first glance, teeters on a knife-edge between banality and danger. We wanted to veer towards the dangerous. We wanted a phantasmagoria of extreme emotions and extraordinary inner landscapes – anything at all that avoided the everyday and the expected.

We need not have worried. The relationship between sons and mothers has inbuilt colour, tension, intensity and drama.

Even though we chose the contributors by instinct, and were in many cases completely in the dark about their personal circumstances, we were hopeful from the beginning that the book would fulfil its ambitious brief. Nevertheless, there were nagging doubts. Would the stories be all the same? Would it all be a terrible anticlimax?

We soon realized that the likelihood of a dull son-and-mother story was very remote. As we put metaphorical pins in maps tracing the latest battle-fronts, the troops in the field were finding out all manner of things about themselves. Some combatants dug in to give themselves the best chance of success, while others temporarily left the field distressed and exhausted.

Who could blame them? Whether sons or mothers, they were approaching the very core of their lives from their different vantage points, and the view was sometimes tragi-comic and nearly always astonishingly painful. But the embattled contributors kept delivering the goods, one by one. And just when it seemed the intensity was too much, there would be some chink of light and a way through discovered. As you will see, we have left our own blood-stained footsteps on the battlefield. But as co-editors and collaborators we have been as one.

Once everything was safely in, some themes became apparent. Fathers were everywhere but nowhere. Fathers and mothers play hugely different roles. The conventional idea of parents as a 'team' in the family seems to be way off-beam in real life. Father may be a source of anxiety, or a balm. But however dominant, or however shadowy or absent the father-figure, his existence provides a necessary ballast to the flights of fantasy and intrigue between mother and son. We were surprised, more prosaically, how much seems to happen in the family car, and how often driving seems emblematic of power. Cars feature more frequently than family pets or teddy bears. And then there is the rather surreal recurrence of hair. Hair is not always what it seems.

We are grateful to our contributors for their courage and clarity. The book has exceeded our initial expectations. All the contributors have put themselves on the line, no doubt cursing frequently that they ever got involved in the first place. Having finally released their writing into the world, we hope they will find satisfaction, pleasure and profit in what they have done. We would like to acknowledge the risks that they took and thank them most sincerely for telling their stories.

MATTHEW GLENDINNING
VICTORIA GLENDINNING

Playing with the Cars

MATTHEW GLENDINNING

Matthew Glendinning was born in Southampton in 1962. He is a freelance sports writer and broadcaster.

Writing about your mother isn't easy. (Nor is writing about your son, as will become evident.) You'd think it would be easier: the narrative is all there, the stories from a lifetime's experience, combining childhood exploits with an adult perspective. But that's only half the story. There's more work to be done. There is the duty you owe to your future, and the attendant consideration of how what is written will affect the future of others. So the key you choose initially isn't necessarily the one you finish in. All the writers, in one way or another, have had to struggle with these conflicting influences, and many have been surprised, as much by the process as by the final outcome. It could always be more difficult: Father Michael Seed, who feels he has had five mothers in his life, told me of an eminent Nigerian bishop who was brought up by twenty mothers. Where would you begin? But even with the one mother it's as though the subject demands you have a cosmic plan. Or you make one up.

Christmas day 1995. Walked with my Mum and her dog round and round a small park near her old house in North Villas. It's a crisp sunny day and my ear-lobes are getting delicately frozen. There's a groovy-looking media couple (must be) doing the rounds too with a big black gambolling young dog attached to a leash. We pass them twice on the circuit. The third time round, they take a detour. 'It's like a board game,' says my mother. And it is, or it's like a game of Scalectrix, toy racing-cars that ran on electrified panels. That was the first big Christmas present my brothers and I got back in the sixties. We frazzled the connecting wires under the bonnets in no time.

My mother has four sons. The others are called Paul, Hugo and Simon, and I'm the third child in between Hugo and Simon. I feel more comfortable placing myself among the brood and for the first sixteen or so years of my life, I feel that's how Mum and I related: I was part of the great scramble of brothers, who needed feeding, taking on holiday and their football kit washed. We all had our own separate moments with Mum, and as we're all into our thirties now, we have formed our own separate visions of her, our own ways and language. Different ways of expressing love; which in my case have veered between great tenderness and other feelings, at times, infuriating and enigmatic.

My mother met my father while he was lecturing at Oxford. Mum was an undergraduate. Her parents were not immediately enamoured of the match but they went ahead and married anyway. Mum had four boys before she was twenty-seven. I remember her as a bright and slightly seductive presence in my life. Once she'd raised us to toddlers, so the story goes, she thought to herself one night when Dad was working: 'What am I going to do now?' And she began to write.

When you are a child you couldn't care less if your mother is a talented writer or not. If you know anything about it at all, which you do intuitively, you'd prefer it if she wasn't. Even now, I am apt to dismiss the fact that she has written things that have captivated other people. In a way, I still couldn't care less, except that it has greatly formed her thinking, her interest in the world, and her independent outlook and circumstances. I've read some of her books and images have stuck in my mind, like that of the frog trying to leap out of a character's cupped hands in *Electricity*. Mum's conversation is sprinkled with metaphors – it's a gift she has – and at dinner parties I enjoy them with everyone else. At other times, I think she has a problem saying things straight: I prefer having dinner with her all to myself. It is then I stop seeing her understanding of things as for the benefit of a wider audience, and realise that her language responds to me and, if anything, I'm the one who becomes playful with words and metaphor just to make her laugh.

But her writing is for your benefit, not mine. When I was five I was told by an au pair girl I wasn't to disturb Mum because she was writing. I toddled up the stairs anyway, and knocked on the door. She said, 'Come in,' and when I did she smiled, and gave me a hug – she was very happy to see me. Even so, I realised there was something mysterious, private and exclusive about this writing business. And it frightened me. I absolutely adored my mother but I wasn't reassured. No amount of reassurance could alter my feeling that there was something going on behind the door that didn't involve me.

When I got a bit older and we were living in Ireland, I found my own domain behind closed doors. I played football with cars till the knees of my trousers wore out. I won't go into the intricacies of the game, but it involved teams of different coloured Matchbox cars, a marble, and two shoe boxes with one side cut out from each box, to make goals, which were positioned at each end of the room. I commentated, as the teams which represented countries – Orange for Holland, Red for England, White for West Germany, Blue for Italy and so on – took part in an ongoing competition. Although I controlled both sides, I had no idea who the winners would be. With such a compelling pastime, it was Mum who had to knock on my door to see if I was coming down for dinner. In fact, when a recent relationship ended, I found myself saying, 'Is the door open or shut?'

This unacknowledged battle is leavened in my memory by more glamorous impressions of the life our family led: moving to Dublin is one of them, holidays in Spain another. Perhaps I loved my mother a bit too much. In Ireland, I can remember a trip to the idyllic Wicklow mountains. At the bottom of a valley I came across a beautiful pale blue quartz-encrusted rock. I hefted it up the hill clasping it to my chest, such was its weight. I think both Mum and Dad wanted to lend me a hand or get me to leave it, but I was obsessive about getting it to the top myself. And when I did I gave it to Mum. The Irish tourist office will have to forgive me for stealing one of Ireland's natural assets, but it has led a charmed life and now resides in the pond of my mother's garden in Kentish Town, amid the lilies and frogspawn. I like the idea that every time Mum's moved house, she's had to ask herself, 'What am I going to do with that rock?'

I think it's around this time, too, that I must have developed my flair for the slightly masochistic romantic gesture: one that future girlfriends will have experienced with varying degrees of pleasure and dismay. At school in Ireland, I fell in love with Naomi Cairns. I wanted to rescue her from a burning classroom. Instead, I handed Naomi her coat at going-home time. She said crossly, 'I can get my own coat.' But it seemed to do the trick. I raided Mum's jewellery box for a gift to give Naomi. It was an ornate silver box with small curved legs that sat on Mum's dressing-table. Inside were pearls, gold and silver chains, rings of all types, and button ear-rings. I can recall it very clearly. Mum had an orb-shaped, psychedelic, plastic ring with the word 'LOVE' floating inside it. I stole it, leaving Mum with the less exotic topaz-coloured plastic ring. I got married to Naomi with the ring in the school woods. But the commitment was hard to take and I was always pushing her away thereafter: another habit I haven't entirely shaken off. I'm not sure Mum quite understands my behaviour even now.

As a kid, I took a narcissistic interest in my looks. Mum loves shiny things and when I was about seven she gave me two shiny shirts, one white, one blue. I think they may have helped in attracting Naomi – at least, that's what my little brother said. I loved them and wore them with pride in the summer. Sport, too, had a narcissistic angle – I felt it showed off the entire effect quite satisfactorily. It was also a skill I could be proud of and gave me recognition among my

brothers and peers – and relief from thought. My brothers
and I were a bunch of pretty boys, with long seventies-style
hair, and golden tans from our long holidays in Spain,
financed and made possible by Dad's university career as a
professor of Spanish. The two-day drives through France to
the Spanish border were sometimes the most enjoyable part
of the trip. We were all crammed into the car together. Dad
did most of the driving but sometimes Mum took over for
brief spells, to the mirth and anxiety of all the brothers. Dad
wasn't comfortable with the change of roles. Mum is a very
good driver, and now I have complete confidence in her
driving, but then my eyes were glued to the road whenever
she took over. It's still a source of hilarity to this day, amid
her indignant protestations that Dad wouldn't give up the
wheel. Mum, you were an unknown quantity as co-driver.
That's all.

One memory from those trips to Spain is particularly keen.
We were looking for a picnic spot off the main roads when we
turned a corner down a country lane, and drove smack into a
gypsy encampment; caravans, Mercedes cars, suspicious stares
and all. Mum grasped Dad's arm with both hands and
breathed urgently, 'Turn around.' Dad performed a dramatic
U-turn with full sound effects. It left an impression on me
because it was an unusually demonstrative moment in front of
the children. We then stopped only two hundred yards down
the road to have our picnic! I thought this was incredibly
cavalier. But at that moment, Mum and Dad, I like to imagine, were blithe and defiant. I was put right off my food
imagining my impending murder.

I know now that Mum took a lot of pride and joy in us.

She's told me that we were regarded as something of a model family. In Spain we swam in the sea and in rivers and played soccer with the local boys. Mum and Dad taught English in the village where we had a house. We spent most days at the beach. Mum had a very delicate way of walking on the sand. I can see her now in her straw hat and bathing-suit, slightly ahead of us, with a carrier bag in one hand containing a book and our innumerable beach things. I wonder what she was thinking. Mum likes to walk now with her delinquent dog, Sophie. It still helps her to think.

My happiest times were spent practising shots with my brother Hugo on the dry grassless *campo de fútbol* in the sun. I don't know what Mum makes of my love of sport. Since she never had a daughter to contrast with her boys, I guess she just accepted it as a gender thing in us. When there are four brothers who like sport, it breeds a feeling of competitive solidarity. During summer holidays after the house in Spain was sold, we would all get in Mum and Dad's double bed to watch the cricket.

So how does it sound so far? Par for the course? Swings and roundabouts? I'm going to have to tell you about cracking up. It was long, it was boring and it had to be done. Walking to the day clinic in Hampstead, I was privy to some strange visual stimulation. All the cars seemed to be red. That is, my eye was constantly being drawn to red cars. I was dressed in shades of Yankee and Confederate blue, which was interesting because I was told that the tightening feeling in my chest was first diagnosed in soldiers about to leave their trenches in the American Civil War. This was a deeply disturbing time for my mother and father, I know, and sensationally and nearly life-threateningly weird for me. Voltaire said, 'Sometimes it's necessary to lose our mind to regain our senses.' I regained mine all right but the battle raged. Funnily enough, it seems preferable to write about this than about my parents' separation when I was an adolescent.

I was still angry with Mum when I went to live with her again in Kentish Town at the age of twenty-four. I had already worn out my loving father. I was in the middle of a process of destruction and deconstruction but at least that made me the protagonist. I put Mum through hell. I know she felt as though she was receiving bruises upon bruises. Moments of light relief were few: in fact the only one I can think of was when my mother and Hugo were sitting in the back garden, drinking gin and tonics on a beautiful summer's evening. I came to join them, and said disingenuously, 'Mum, I hate you.' Mum replied, 'Oh,' in a matter-of-fact way, rather as if a five-year-old had informed her sweetly that he'd been sick on the carpet.

At this time of my life, I was helped by family and friends who cared for me, and especially a psychotherapist, a friend, who saw through all my ruses and all the false structures I'd created for myself. I don't think she knew what she was taking on when she first met me – I certainly didn't – but she was patient and persevered. She was generous and taught me how to listen.

With the encouragement of everyone who counted, I then went to art school. I was lucky. My parents funded me and wanted me to follow my passion. It was an important moment in my relationship with Mum. In my adult life, I had used writing as the primary form of expression – in effect, my mother-language – but now I was learning a new language; one that I could channel straight from my heart. It's a language I value to this day. It is complex but without the linear grammatical rules of prose writing, so it gave me freedom. The American poet and writer Raymond Carver, whom I admire, quoted this principle from Ezra Pound, whom I've never read, and don't particularly like the thought of: 'Fundamental accuracy of statement is the ONE sole morality of writing.' Well, at the time I would have thought, 'You can keep that for the birds.' I didn't want to express anything accurately. I just wanted to express a sensibility. My feeling was: 'It may or may not be good, but that's how it is.'

To make a gesture or a mark on the page seemed as natural as throwing a stone in a pond to make ripples, and far less clichéd. And yet my notebook was still covered with the scrawl of writing, except it was written in charcoal. It's a relief to have up my sleeve an art form that doesn't compare with Mum's work. It's like that with poetry. I don't know why Mum doesn't write poems. And just to square the circle, I think that's one of the reasons why I enjoy sports writing too. As far as I know, my mother hasn't written much on sport, except to use the terminology of snooker for her own metaphorical ends. Maybe she's ghost-written a Gazza autobiography. I'd like to see that up for the literary prizes.

While I was at art school I lived in west London and didn't see much of Mum. I needed to reinvent myself. When I'd gone to university six years earlier, Mum had said, 'Find yourself a sensible dark-haired northern girl.' I appreciated that, but at art school I found a French girl. That Christmas, I was with the family and life was suddenly full of possibilities.

In typically audacious style, Mum had annexed the basement of the house next door. I day-dreamed the afternoon away on a full Christmas lunch in the guest room, thinking of the girl, who wanted me to write to her. Mum eventually sold her house, but now I live in the old annexe, which is where I'm writing this. Mum has helped me out a lot. By the way, it didn't work with the French girl and I never have gone out with a dark-haired northern girl. My next love came from the southern hemisphere.

I got drunk with Mum last night. Not a spectacularly clever thing to do while I'm writing this, but perhaps it will tell me something. My mother got married again in 1981 to the Irish writer Terence de Vere White. Terence died two years ago. Mum's parents, my grandparents, had died in a car crash not long before. In the end, although Terence was much loved, it was a relief for everyone because he was so very ill. Mum had somehow found a way to look after him, remain sane, finish off her Trollope biography and then write the novel *Electricity*. She has a very strong pysche and a practicality and acceptance in the face of catastrophe. It helps that her life-imagination and instinct for self-preservation are particularly deep-rooted. I'm sure Terence wouldn't mind me saying this, but the period since his death has created space. It's been my time with Mum. I'm still not exactly sure what to do with it but it has allowed me to get closer to her and many other good things.

Writing this and sharing the duties of editing this book have created some unusual situations. We had been shadowing each other to see what the other was thinking or about to write, so we went to see the film *Babe* together on a Sunday afternoon. It was meant to be a distraction, but since I've only been to see one film before with Mum in recent years, it was quite an occasion. The other time was over ten years ago, to see *Salvador*. At that time, I feared the intimacy of seeing a film together might prove overwhelming. Mum was reviewing the film for radio or a newspaper. I sensed her purposefulness, and her pleasure in my company and as a consequence I enjoyed myself. *Babe* was a different story. The expedition took about four days to coordinate, so by the time she drove me up to Hampstead there was an element of light farce about it. I said on the way there, 'Drive safely, Mum. We may get through this *Babe* experience in one piece.'

I was half expecting to regress to the age of about five, and was relieved when Mum said afterwards that she had felt like a child. I had assumed the role of a grudgingly amused teenager who eventually chilled out.

She said on the way home, 'Well, that was surprisingly easy, given all we went through to get there!'

"Did you cry?' I said.

'Yes, but it's easy for me to cry.'

'I was manipulated to tears, especially when all that cheering started, and then got EVEN louder . . .'

Mum said at least she'd be able to talk about it at a party she was going to that night.

'I'm going to have a fry-up when I get home,' I said. 'The plump backside of Babe, and all that see-through, short-haired skin just made me think of bacon.'

'Well, it wasn't worth all the noise about it, was it?' she continued.

'No, but this guy I know wrote an article saying that a lot

of Australian films are about acceptance of the outsider, or of being different because it's a young country. That's why the farmer and the pig are accepted at the end.'

Mum liked the old farmer. The voices were changed for the Anglo-American audience. Mum thought: 'Maybe it would have had more chutzpah if the animals had had Australian voices.'

'I can't believe the pig was a re-dubbed voice. I think the sheep were Irish, weren't they?'

Ma said, 'I think all the voices were re-dubbed.'

'Nah, definitely not the sheep.'

The bad days are over. I don't want to punish Mum. I want to take her out to dinner. The first proper dinner we shared was at the Groucho Club at about the same time as *Salvador*. I must have been excitable because I ordered sheep's brains. God knows what we talked about. 'What was I going to do next?' seems a fair guess. But I can remember everything else very clearly: the huge pastel-coloured painting in the dining-room and the clean, white-shirted elegance of the waitresses. I couldn't manage the sheep's brains but I can still feel its experimental warmth in my mouth. So it was warm, in pastel colours with white-shirted refinement, and I probably felt at the time that I could do with a lot more of this, although without the sheep's brains. We go out for lunch or dinner quite often now. Each one means something to me.

Now it's time to return to my brothers. The youngest and eldest have both made careers in academia: Paul is a mathematician and Simon a philosopher. Hugo and I, in the middle, have taken after Mum and are involved in the media – Hugo's a photographer and I'm a sports writer. Mum wants the four of us to have our own TV show. We have all gravitated back to live near our parents: Simon lives near Mum, and Hugo and Paul live or work near Dad in the East End. They have lived further away than I have from Mum in recent years, and perhaps they have a clearer perspective – or at least, they have formed their own view of her in an unshakeable way. But I doubt it. You never really know who the other person is, so there's always room for surprises. There are many things I don't want to know about Mum, and a million things we could talk about. As far as I'm concerned, it's only the listening and the being together that seem to count. If there is 'a comedy to being a son' it is that whatever you do, whatever you achieve, whatever loves you hold and throw away in your life, your mother still thinks of you as her child. Sometimes that's just as well.

My brothers and I like to bring her gifts: gifts of creation, success, thought and humour. Mum has a clear understanding of what it takes to strive for something with determination and against the odds. Her first book, *A Suppressed Cry*, was a biography based on the letters of a distant relative who lived in Victorian times and whose creativity and intelligence were stifled to death by a patriarchal society. The book moved me greatly, and I think is partly the story of Mum's compassion for the sides of herself that needed expression and weren't heard when she was a child. For my part, I am learning to understand her talents, and even to reappraise the level of commitment, competence and imagination it takes to write a book. It would be a waste if I didn't. I know that my brothers and I value her achievements and energy, and above all else her companionship. We also appreciate her courage in the way she has continued to immerse herself in life while mourning Terence.

She respects the obsessions we have turned into careers. She also loves and respects the girlfriends and wives who have attached themselves to us. Mum is a powerful and pivotal figure in their affections too. Mum is a feminist and it was her fate to have four boys! We have brought her all kinds of unlikely gifts but our girlfriends would be high up on her list. But none of us has helped make her a grandmother – yet.

I think she's still a bit surprised her grown-up sons may need her. Perhaps she thought that men just got on with it. I still get frustrated when she sees the female view first and not the feelings I'm trying to get to grips with, but I also think she has learnt from us. I know she loves us. We, I, love her too. When I struggled to breathe with tonsillitis last year, Mum took me to hospital and kept me company as I gasped for breath in an NHS waiting-room. She came to see me every day. I couldn't eat and I was on a drip. I looked more and more like St Francis of Assisi. I couldn't talk for four days but I wrote things down to her. After some gruesome details of liquid-filled tonsils, I wrote: 'But he [Martin Amis] never really knew these guys in the first place. You imagine him with his half of lager in a pub taking notes – maybe this is a bit cruel.' Mum asked if she could use that in her review! I like that. Mum rarely misses a trick. As one of my brothers' girlfriends said to me, 'She's a liver,' and she didn't mean as opposed to a kidney. Mum is interested in all aspects of life, and gets from it all she can.

But I don't want to leave this with an image of myself on a sick-bed and my mother, the ministering angel. I couldn't even if I wanted to. There are still unresolved emotions from way back to be addressed in our relationship. It saddened me when we first exchanged these articles to see that some feelings were still so prominent, and have evidently not left her. Things got a little complicated: the present can feel like another country when you write about and then read about your own past. But there's time to sort out the real issues. It's not as though what is written in 1996 is the last word.

This Christmas my father came round to Mum's house to share dinner with the family for the first time in twenty years. I was expecting my mother to be coquettish and my father to be reserved but it was very relaxed. In fact, it went off beautifully. They took their time. And now this story has loomed and passed like a whale I'm going to take my time as well.

JILL DAWSON

Jill Dawson was born in 1962 in Durham and grew up in Yorkshire. She is a poet, novelist and short-story writer, editor of The Virago Book of Love Letters *and* The Virago Book of Wicked Verse. *She lives in Hackney with her son.*

P æ a n

to my child
with his tiny
pod of a penis

O, how I love to
smother it in kisses,
douse it with vanilla talc:
that butter-pale catkin
of downy-soft skin.

His clear yellow urine
– I'm not taking the piss –
only meaning to praise:
     smallness
     friendliness.

O, at last, to *love*
not to envy it
– which has deflowered no one,
penetrated nothing, caused
no more offence than
a chipolata sausage. Uncooked.

To think,
all were button mushrooms once,
every last one
sweet and temperate.
Such monuments I would make to it!
The Buds of Stonehenge,
Cleopatra's Thimble,
the Eiffel Thumb.

O, but how my son
will curse me, at twenty
reading this.
So proud will he be
of his grown-up
        penis.

W ig

JON SNOW

*Jon Snow was born in 1947. He grew up in Sussex,
when his father was a public school headmaster, and in
Yorkshire, where his father was a Bishop. His mother,
Joan, was born in 1910. He has been a journalist since
1973, currently with Channel Four News.*

'Boys, there's something I think you ought to know about
your mother.' As so often, my father was talking to the rear-
view mirror of his beloved 1931 Hudson Terraplane Eight.
His three sons were arrayed on the back seat in matching pale
blue cable-stitch mother-knitted sweaters. She was sitting with
her back to us in the front seat. There was a long pause as he
negotiated the huge convertible round another Dorset bend
too fast. 'Your mother doesn't have her own hair,' he said
finally.

The silence that followed was eventually broken by my
elder brother snootily announcing, 'I knew that.' But I didn't,
and at eight years old I was utterly shattered. I simply could-
n't begin to make sense of it. 'Didn't you even know, Jobby?'
My elder brother, using the sneering nickname by which he

got under my skin, clearly sensed my shock. 'I've always known,' he added. My younger brother, at six, was reticent about being seen to be as candid as my tears began to reveal me to be, or as cocky as his eldest brother now boasted.

'Yes, darlings, I haven't had any hair since I was a girl,' chimed my mother. 'Your father was absolutely wonderful ever to marry me.' So, I thought, this hairlessness had been a most terrible and unmentionable thing. And curiously, right up until adult life it was to remain a most terrible and unmentionable thing. From henceforth it was rarely touched upon, other than in the most oblique references.

At some point, soon after that car journey, we three boys did discuss it from the same stances in which the initial revelation had left us. My elder brother, Tom, stated that as a consequence of attending the school of which my father was head, he'd been persistently teased and bullied by other boys who knew, and who had made cruel fun of my mother's wig. She suffered, it seemed, from *alopecia totalis*. At thirteen she had lost her hair in a night while sitting a piano exam. And that was that.

But for me it wasn't. Very suddenly Mummy wasn't quite the same Mummy. I was left to return to boarding-school wondering who this new, hairless Mummy was. Nothing had prepared me. I'd never for one moment wondered whether the hair on her head was real. I had taken it upon absolute trust that it was. That it now wasn't, somehow undermined my entire confidence in who she really was.

My earliest life with her had been interlaced with a life with Nanny. Nanny was a very down-to-earth, giggly woman, who had not an ounce of sensuality about her. She was practical, dependable and devoid of complication. My mother, on the other hand, was complicated from the start. Bleak were the Thursday evenings when Nanny had her half-day. Bath-time was utter chaos on such evenings as my mother battled to get us all washed and to bed.

Nanny would wash our hair on Fridays and we would lie on towels in front of the fierce glowing elements of the old-fashioned gas-fire in my mother's bedroom. These were the very rare occasions when we were allowed into her room. She would be there too, sitting close by, sometimes assisting the drying with a towel. I remember lying there, looking up her legs and wanting to see her in the nude – but I never did. Looking back, it's obvious why I never did. For in those days, her door was hooked closed at night, with a two-inch gap so that she could hear us if we called out. My father had wired it up to prevent us pushing the door any further open. Sometimes the door was bolted shut altogether. Beyond those treasured moments in front of the gas-fire, I have no memory of any other tactile life with her. I did not sit on her lap, nor ever run my fingers through her hair, as my own children do mine. Kisses were an endurance – perfunctory, charged with nothing. And yet I was conscious of being the apple of her eye.

Although I don't remember it, I was breast-fed. I recall once finding the glass equivalent of an old car hooter, which Tom reliably informed me had been used to help my mother feed me. My earliest memories are of a sun-kissed life sitting under the wattled shadow of the loggia in the garden, with the white tassels of the sunshade above my little brother Nick's pram blowing in the breeze. Ice clinked in a bulbous glass jug

of Rose's lime juice. My father and mother toiled in the garden; Nanny busied herself with us.

Winters were cold beyond the bedroom gas-fires and the
roaring open log fire in the drawing-room. The stairs and
landings were of scrubbed stone, the bedroom floors of blue
lino; only the drawing-room floor was of warm oak, strewn
with carpets. It was the black Blüthner boudoir grand against
one wall that was the biggest statement of my mother's existence. A vast Voight loudspeaker system, which looked like a
tasteful ice-cream kiosk – my father's pride and joy – was the
other competing presence.

The piano was the thread of contact with my mother that
wove through my childhood. She was a wondrously bold per-
former, in stark contrast to the retiring role that she otherwise
played within the family. Her long, slender, beautifully nailed
fingers spreadeagled powerfully across the notes as she played
her beloved Brahms. She didn't play often, and never without
sheet music – I longed for her to extemporise and touch
some of the tunes I knew. So instead, from perhaps the age of
four, I began to pick up themes from her playing and hum or
sing along with her. I was alone in this and concerned that my
more macho brothers would tease me for it. But gradually I
began to sing with more gusto. It was in this single activity
that my mother revealed her most demonstrative maternal
delight. Her engagement ring would clink about on the
ivories, as I, who could only vaguely decipher the clusters of
notes on the page, waited for the nod that would signal me to
turn it.

But once the music stopped I would resist her enthusiasm
and praise, feeling somehow embarrassed about this singular

special link with her. From this seed sprang a lifelong sense from her that in some way I was different from the other boys – my brothers and my father. Once, later in life, she told me shyly that I was the nearest thing to the daughter she never had. The trauma of hair-loss left a need in her to confide, and so far as I know, that need has never been requited.

We grew up in a home dominated by my huge father. Six foot seven, with fine large hands, he was an eternal practical activist. The house was strewn with gadgets. The workshop was the centre of his world. Jars and neatly labelled tins of hooks, nuts, bolts, switches, solenoids, valves and rubber bands were set on cascades of shelves around a room that smelled for ever of Durafix. My mother was not of this workshop world in any form. My two brothers were. I was not.

My mother knitted – there was always a pullover on the go, often for me. I would paint with water-colours, at which she too was proficient. I remember when I was five my father deciding to paint the lumbering caravan that was kept in the garden for our summer holidays. I wanted to help. I set about mixing up and matching what I thought to be the right green for the hub-caps. My father deployed himself on the grand painting of the caravan's sides. Suddenly his eye lighted upon my efforts. 'I say,' he called out to my mother, 'is this mess ever going to come off, Joan?' She and I were somehow to blame for my well-intentioned desire to get involved. I felt safe in her reassurance to my father that it was only water-colour, but let down that the wheels were not to remain adorned by my tiny brush-strokes. When he suggested I apply myself to a block of wood nearby, she understood that was no substitute for the wheels.

Thus, in those early days, when my brothers joined him in the workshop I would look for alternatives. My father saw me as a DIY non-starter; my mother saw me as musical and more sensitive than I really was. Her faith in me began to channel itself towards developing my music. One day at breakfast my father called out from behind *The Times*. He had found an ad for voice trials to select choristers for Winchester Cathedral. And so began an intensive few weeks of arpeggios, harmonics, musical theory and my selected offering, 'Oh Little Town of Bethlehem'. These were the prerequisites for the voice trials. My mother was determined to get me through.

The consequences of her efforts were revealed in the autumn when we turned out, hollow-tummied with nerves, for the long journey in the Hudson to my first term in Winchester. I was seven and completely unprepared for the separation that was to come.

'You'll have to take a tough line with him – he can't even tie his own shoe-laces.' My father was issuing instructions to the headmaster of the choir school. I was being hustled into the arms of the man's waiting wife. I called over my shoulder to my mother, 'Don't go until I've said goodbye, will you?' 'I won't,' she said. Half an hour later, I asked to go back and see her. 'Oh, she's gone already,' I was informed.

In that instant, the heart-broken, bereft, but independent new me was born. The umbilical was finally broken. For months at a time, the only signal that I had a mother was the arrival in the mail of pale blue Basildon Bond envelopes. They were emblazoned with my mother's bold blue Quink ink handwriting. Her letters were a constant throughout my schooling, but they never told me much, and never anything of her feelings.

The closeness of my contact with my mother was undermined still further by the fact that my singing duties necessitated staying on for saints' days and religious festivals, long after other boarding-school children had gone home for the holidays. A week after Christmas and another at Easter were all I got as holidays at home. The first few days at home after long terms were stiff and formal re-entry processes. My mother displayed emotion only when we reached platform seven at Waterloo Station for the journey back to school. Those partings, despite the drift in our relationship, perhaps because of it, were always painful.

The summer holidays were different. For a full month we would camp in sun-drenched cornfields in Dorset. My father used to bring most of the contents of his workshop with him, and life was a succession of highly ordered and annually repeated events. Huge haulage operations accompanied any visit to the beach. Most of the tarpaulin for a hay-rick and five great poles would be trussed up on the Hudson, together with picnic baskets, chairs and the rest. Only later did I realise that the tarpaulin, erected to provide a kind of corral against the winds, was there to protect my mother's hair from lift-off. Most days she'd have a Jaqumar scarf tied under her chin. When she swam, it was in a tight rubber bathing-cap. Although the scarf struck me as 'different' at the time, I never queried why she wore it so much at the beach.

The high spot of this month by the sea was 27 August, my mother's birthday. Like so much else in our family life, this was a circus of an event, but one in which I could see and understand the true extent of my awkward father's love for her. It was a day in which references were often made to events before we were born. In retrospect, her utter gratitude to him for marrying her forged perhaps the strongest inter-dependence between two people I have ever seen. Only on that day was she anything other than my father's subservient creature. This was the day upon which, from the moment we woke, she was queen. Wild flowers would have been picked, presents packed and piled, and we would watch as she undid items bought with love but ultimately targeted, for the most part, at impersonal needs. A Poole pottery butter dish, a weird nut-cracker, another Liberty scarf, were the staple diet. They were accompanied by none of the Blue Grass toilet water and cashmere sweaters she could really have done with. This was the only day in the year when she was the centre of our attention.

It was in my second year at the choir school that matron suddenly informed me that my father was coming to see me. He never came without Joan. There was good reason for his solitary arrival. She was in hospital, badly cut about the face from a car crash. For some reason he had panicked that I might have found out through the private school grape-vine. In some way this accident, because of cuts around her pen-cilled eyebrows, revealed her hairlessness more definitively. It was this that tripped the subsequent blunt revelation through the Hudson's rear-view mirror.

After the shock of discovery a lot of things did begin to fit into place. My mother, in the rare oblique references she ever made to her wig, called it 'Ab'. Absolom's biblical misfortune, which left him hanging from a branch by his hair, provided the verbal disguise that she required. I now understood what the occasional strong, perfect cardboard box from Isaacs of Sloane Street contained. Down the years, in the post there had been a slow succession of such boxes, which we brothers had fantasised might be presents. Now we knew. I'm not sure whether she got them on the NHS. But in later life she did reveal that she could not afford one as a child, and had to wear a bonnet to school. The awful bullying and sadness she must have suffered were never mentioned. Not until she was eighteen had her elder brother found the funds to buy her a wig.

All this contributed to the retreating person that as a mother she seems to have been. In company, especially formally, she seems to have been able to play a confident wifely role. She had met, become engaged to, and married my father in six wartime weeks. At thirty-three, she had never had a man before. At forty, he had never had a woman. This mutual collision of need seems to have been marred only by the fact that my father, too, had never noticed her wig. After he'd asked her to marry him she told him of it. He needed twenty-four hours to think about it. It was twenty-four hours in which she decided her life would be dedicated to his every beck and call, providing he would have her.

There was never any doubt in my mind, as a child, that he came first. Nothing was more important than his well-being. He was the hourly priority. Thus as a mother, although she was always there, she was not easily confided in. Preoccupied with who her husband was, she was judgemental and inflexible in her view of who her boys were. Throughout my childhood she regarded me as a far more saintly, generous and kindly person than I knew myself to be. I hated it, and hated the constant 'that's just not like you' comments that would accompany some piece of my behaviour that did not fit with her picture of me.

I was very shocked when I saw her after the car crash. I had not been allowed home to visit her in hospital. I saw her only some three weeks after the event. The accident had been caused by a classic misperformance by my father. The alternator had gone on the car, and he'd been trying to drive home in the dark. He missed a sharp bank and turned the vehicle over, throwing my mother out through the windscreen. He did not appear chastened by it, nor to notice my mother's immediate but temporary disfigurement. But I was now transfixed by her wig. I wondered what she looked like bald. Did she sleep in it? Did she have hair between her legs? They were a child's questions that were never answered.

I began to look at every grown woman's head, to see if she too had a wig. This became a brief obsession in the choir stalls at Winchester. I had always studied the scattered souls who turned out for services. Now I inspected them in great detail. Then one Sunday night I spotted a wig. For sure it was a wig. You could see up the neck – there were no wisps linking the blond hair on top with the nape. The woman was fifteen feet away. She began to swim in front of my eyes, I swayed and fainted softly on to the stone cathedral floor. I had no explanation for those who asked me why I had fainted. Somehow I doubt now that it was a wig at all.

Gradually the wig interest subsided. Life with Mummy settled back into the old relatively distant routine. But in hindsight, I think the handling of it affected my entire relationship with her.

I have no real memory of early adolescence with my mother. Sex was absolutely never referred to. She was a keen observer of the post-bag in my mid-teens, but few of the young women I occasionally danced with at awkward adolescent parties ever wrote. Later she was an intolerant receiver of any woman Tom or I might bring into the house. I studied *Sons and Lovers* at A level and recognised my mother's resentful attitude in its pages. Taking a woman home was simply not a good idea. So by eighteen the distance between us had widened to a gulf. When I first became consumed by a woman – a twenty-year-old Swiss waitress at a sixth-form conference – I could not discuss it, even though I know she knew, and had probably found a photo in my room to confirm it.

I began to live a life in which she was never present as a force. At nineteen I cast away to Uganda to teach on VSO for a year, and wrote home every week. Each letter was an exercise in story-telling in which there was no feeling. There was no revelation of things that really mattered, certainly not of the sweet Ugandan probationer teacher I kissed upon the Nile.

By the time I returned home at twenty, the transition in my relationship with Mum was complete. The piano ivories had long been stilled, the commonalities of our life were over. Although I retained a loved room within the family house, I had left home for good. At twenty-three, even the room went. They moved and now there was only a house, in which I had never lived, to visit. Such visits were sparse and claustrophobic. For in this house in which I had no room, there was no escape. She now had a life which had reconnected with that which had predated her sons' existence. She longed to see me, could hardly contain her joy upon my arrival. But that was where it ended. It became fun to assume extreme political stances to reassure her that I was still an abiding shit and not the saintly boy she had loved. She too was not above a bitchy aside about some person she knew to be of importance to me.

Boarding-school, Uganda, her insecurities around the wig, her obsession with my father, made any chance of constructing some new mid-life relationship with her impossible.

During this time of recognition of the distance between son and mother, her old boy died, and with him her life. He had gone out for a sunset walk to his favourite spot above the castled Dorset village in which they lived, and just died. My father's dog sat beside his body, silhouetted on the skyline, as my mother and the village policeman came up to find him. Arriving late that night, we three brothers were suddenly thrown closer together with her. We talked easily in our loss. His signet ring, ten coins, his absurd portable tool-kit, a paper-clip and a note-pad lay painfully on the table – the contents of his pockets, returned by the police.

My mother's only true love was dead. None of us could replace him. She was sixty-seven and bereft. By the time he died he'd become a bishop – there was something symbolically final about his episcopal cope and mitre laid out across his huge coffin. He was definitely in there.

How early the Alzheimer's began to take hold of her is impossible to say. I feel that the trauma of my father's death may have had a similar effect upon her to that early piano exam for the Royal College of Music, which had triggered her alopecia. I think I can find signs of her deterioration throughout the last nineteen or twenty years.

But the early months of her widowhood were a return to the best of childhood, as long as Tom or Nick was there to share it. I still found her claustrophobic on her own. Tom would question her most directly about the past and at times she would talk quite freely. But there were dark recesses – a 'black Friday', and a 'black Wednesday' upon which some indescribable incident had occurred within her married life. We discovered she had lost her first baby, though again we could not divine whether the baby was stillborn or died during birth or soon after.

In those days, and a little later too, I glimpsed something of what I had missed in not achieving a closer relationship with her. In the year of two dead Popes, 1978, the year after my father's death, I was posted to Rome. I decided to try to get my mother out to Italy for Christmas. Combining the need to have her accompanied on her flight with my reluctance to have her stay for long with me on my own, I persuaded my younger brother to come with her. She had hardly ever been abroad, and never without my father. Christmas night mass found this conservative Protestant bishop's widow standing on a chair in St Peter's, shouting and waving at the new John Paul II. Fortunately she was not alone; a good number of Roman Catholics were at it too. In those few days there was a hint of exuberance and fun that she had hardly ever let loose in our earliest lives.

We took her up to Siena and Assisi. She did all the things she would love to have done much earlier in life. She bought an improbable white china dove, life-size. It was an ornament my father would not have had in the house. But at last her own taste was beginning to prevail.

At home she moved again, to a smaller house within the same village. Five years after my father died, my first daughter, my mother's second granddaughter, was born. My visits to see Mum, never very plentiful, became more scarce. My own child scrambling about on my chest quickly underlined how starkly different relationships had been in my own beginnings. An early visit by Granny accentuated the matter still further. She was exasperated by the baby and strangely incapable of adjusting to her needs. But this may have been another gestation signal from the Alzheimer evil.

Keys, and where she'd parked the car, became the touchstones of her mental state. Ten years ago she began locking herself out of her house. She would also park in Station Road and then forget while doing the shopping. The police began to spend increasing amounts of time helping her to track down her car. But because she lived on her own in a cautious, conservative community, months went by without any serious mention of what was happening. My visits were so sparse that I was able to detect changes in the physical well-being of the house. I had very little idea about dementia or Alzheimer's itself. It was her neighbours, both much older than my mother, who bore the brunt of what was happening to her. At first they were desperate to help her stay where she wanted, in her own home. Finally, five years ago, after a succession of chaotic adventures, we decided she would have to move.

Oblivious of the gravity of her true condition, we set out to find the most beautiful local surroundings, mindful to couple them with the 'right kind' of inmate. We came up with two wonderful homes. She was out of the first in a night, and out of the second in two. Suddenly she was incarcerated in the open public ward of Poole General, on drugs. She changed before our eyes. The geriatricians were quick in their diagnosis of mild dementia and Alzheimer's and said we had to have her out and housed in a fortnight.

Perhaps if our life together had prepared us and left us with a living friendship, I might have tried. But, as it had not, I was ruthless in my refusal to make sacrifices to care for her. Guilt wrestled with reality, as each of her sons trundled across Britain in search of a viable old people's home. All over the country we met similar sons and daughters facing similar conflicts. The provision was ghastly, almost universally. The smell of incontinence battling with the odour of detergents hung in my nostrils long after the day's researches were over. Finally in panic, a grisly Gothic country house, smartly painted, smoothly managed, locked its front door behind her. We hung photos of her old boy, and the grandchildren she couldn't cope with, on her walls. We squeezed in her old desk and most-loved chair, to make her feel at home, and away we went.

Mummy was now effectively locked away. Emotionally within me she had died. One hour visiting her in that home was worse than any whole weekend had ever been.

We were rescued by a small home in Oxfordshire, widely regarded as one of the few specialist units in the country, for which there had been a lifetime's waiting-list. Somehow a place came up. She is there to this day. When I walk in, she knows me instantly. But there is no conversation, no thread, no continuity, no friendship. Physically shrunken, she still has the poise and intonation of the bishop's wife, still has the demeanour of my mother. But it is a physical thing frozen in time. Mentally mother and son have stopped. It feels brutal and laden with guilt, but to look at it any other way would be to invent something that simply is not there.

When she dies, my thoughts of her will wake up and cry.

Poor Mum, what a hard life and lingering, difficult death. And what has this son's time with this mother left in the son? Gratitude for the music and the security of the start; a pathological fear of claustrophobic relationships with women, perhaps; an acute reluctance to risk real closeness; a passion and capacity to live life to the full; a hatred of the subjugation of a woman that probably still doesn't quell in me a capacity to subjugate; and an appreciation of the openness, touch, friendship and love that eluded so much of my relationship with her.

A B o y in t h e F a m i l y

SOPHIE PARKIN

Sophie Parkin, born in 1961, is a King's Road baby, Art School Product, Night Club Manager, Performing Poet, Artist, Novelist. She now lives in London writing and broadcasting, and is the proud mother of Paris (9) and Carson (6). She is currently working on a play and The Knowledge, *a definitive life-guide for the year 2000.*

'Paris, I could call my son Paris, if I ever had a son,' I thought, as I gazed, mesmerised by the beauty of the bronze hero in the tacky auction room. I was six months pregnant and certain I would never have a boy. I was too busy to dwell on it, too eager feathering our nest till it looked like an overstuffed cushion, in preparation for the baby. I bid for the bust, it went too high and we ended up with a claw-footed bath instead, a must-have for our eighties' Hackney bathroom. But I unintentionally stole the name home with me. How did I know that at age five he would plead for a name 'more unusual, like John'?

The baby was very much planned, longed for and loved, but all of those feelings didn't take away the strangeness. I'd done all sorts of things in my growing up and now I was this woman, this full-tummied woman, filled with baby, my baby and 'our baby' but mostly, secretly, mine. In its early days I fed it on a diet of wine and cigarette smoke until official, then I exchanged the toxins for a negligible nutritious balance of peanut butter sandwiches, hot chocolate and milky coffees. Later, I was forced to switch to caffeine-free camomile tea to calm those footballing feet. I should have guessed.

I rang my mama with my joyous news, who cried with excitement at the prospect of the first grandchild (on either side of the family), before going out to get drunk for four days and four nights, before giving up alcohol for good.

I rang my papa who took it all very lightly. 'Jolly good show,' he said in a non-committal kind of way. I wasn't convinced he'd heard, but it wasn't unlike every conversation we ever held. Relations with my father at that time weren't strained, they were obsolete. The fact I wasn't married didn't thrill my father, I could tell. The fact that his first grandchild would be a 'bastard' was something I carelessly hadn't even considered. This after all was the eighties.

What mattered most was that I loved this baby and so did its father, Alastair. We wanted this baby and with its presence I was charged with a new fearlessness and courage, the kind that poured out of the ground and up into the soles of my feet every time I touched it. Normally, shoes got in the way, but not this time. Steel toe-caps would have turned into metal cauliflower colanders with this life-force inside me.

Abraham Lincoln couldn't have convinced me that it wasn't right.

I could never have imagined how it would feel to have a baby grow inside me. I was still a child wanting to be cared for. Sometimes, it felt as though I were harbouring an alien roaming about my entrails as in a seventies schlock horror movie; sometimes, as if an older-aged wisdom had ley-lined me for initiation into a real life and another world.

I didn't know it would be a boy, that there could be a boy growing inside me. I assumed it would be a girl: there were only ever girls in my family. My parents had made up for it by always sending me to co-ed schools, but I still felt as ignorant as a nun about boys and their ways. Of course there was my father, but he had been gone for such a time as to empty any real knowledge of males from my psyche. And there was my stepfather, but he was as he was and taught me more of other things. My stepbrothers appeared from when I was nine, on alternate weekends, and just seemed strange with their action men, science fiction and never wanting to have baths. Boys at my schools were playthings, laugh objects, to be teased mercilessly for our sick girl delight. Later, I had boys as friends, but they were different from the boys I had sex with. They were nice, without the cruel mystery and attraction.

What did I know of this boy breed? Nothing.

I was a girl and I would give birth to a girl, my baby, and I would dress her in frou-frous and frills, this is what would happen. Already I was making Joan Crawford-style mother-and-daughter matching outfits for the day of her arrival. Together we would leave the hospital in copy-cat black, red and purple velvets; only the handbags were missing.

Mothercare's soft matching pastels would never touch my daughter's skin. She would be the beneficiary of at least five generations of Welsh witchery, and her grooming in that matriarchal tradition was imperative. My girl was too extraordinary to be called Jane (my birth-certificate name). She would be called Morgan, the name of my ancestors.

The birth was difficult. How could it not be with the fear of all that unknown – pain, life, child, joy. The doctors threaded a needle to gush numbness through my spine, but instead of working it grazed my central nervous system raw. I felt my body elevate off the birthing table and from a far-away corridor heard a scream as primal as death flooding out of my mouth. I raced through my pain threshold faster than the speed of sound, as the doctors rushed from the room anxious not to be implicated in my paralysis or death from their incompetence. Later, a midwife returned to strap my exhausted body to a machine.

'If we don't pull the poor mite out this minute, the baby will be dead,' I heard her lyrical West Indian voice say – was it to me, to Alastair or just to the nurse next to her? A second of relief drifted to my pained brain taking in the slow-motion detail. Brilliant, I thought. They'll have to knock me out from this intolerable agony and give me a Caesarean. A blow to the head with a hammer would have done me fine at that point. Luck wasn't with me, but it was with my baby. The midwife thought on her feet, pulled out a pair of scissors and, quickly cutting my vagina from one end to the other, started screaming at me, 'PUSH!'

My baby arrived shockingly alive and, a BOY? I felt more

like the abandoned cocoon of this new beautiful butterfly, patterned with blood and white mucus, than the mother of anything.

'Are you sure?' I said.

She turned him around on his umbilical cord to show me and then snipped him away to examine his perfect body. Fingers? Ten. Toes? Ten. Breathing? Yes, thank God. They even dressed him and put his first nappy on while I finished giving birth to the mass of livery afterbirth twice the size of my boy. No wonder everyone asked if I was having twins, I thought, peering at the purple red blubber appearing from between my legs. A doctor arrived to examine me and the baby. He didn't address a single word to me, just delved with his hands between my legs before plunging his needle full of belated anaesthetic into me.

'Nurse,' he barked, 'you know very well that it is illegal to perform an episiotomy without an anaesthetic.'

'I didn't have time, doctor.'

'There's always time.'

'The baby had gone into trauma.'

'The hospital can get sued. Let's hope the patient won't prosecute. Get her to sign a form.' He finished the fifteen stitches and turned to the baby before stating, 'Looks fine to me. Nothing missing.'

The midwife handed this live, red-faced, towelling lump to me, placing his small male mouth to my colostrum-yellow, leaking nipples. My throat constricted hard and relieved tears roller-coasted relentlessly down my broken-veined cheeks, like summertime in Blackpool.

I don't care how many babies are born a minute in the

world. This boy was mine and the only one that mattered. A divine miracle. The ceaseless miracle, of life and birth and death. I felt as old as Wookey Hole and about as attractive, and as young as my new baby. I was twenty-five, no, just twenty-six – my birthday had come and gone during the labour. The new-born alien gnawing at my breast for sustenance was my son. He was without any doubt the most beautiful thing I had ever seen. His small wrinkled head, pulled into a Martian deformity by his monitored delivery, expanded my heart up through the sixth layer of my skin until it burst with a waterfall of love flooding my senses. My baby, Paris. What Helen wouldn't willingly leave a thousand Menelauses for this miracle boy? I was in love and none of the rest mattered.

Getting used to the practicalities of having a baby was hard, getting used to a boy even harder. I worried, looking at him, how I would cope. I was frightened by my lack of male understanding, from cleaning his body to interpreting his needs. I had never before spent so much time and energy on somebody else's needs, and he exhausted me with his constant demands for food, attention, cleaning and changing: the baby treadmill. Even after the first few weeks had gone by, I was still debilitated from the birth, with semi-paralysis down my left leg and enough stitches to hold a blanket together. It was a major triumph to have bathed and dressed myself by the time evening had rolled on from morning. Food didn't get a look in, except for Paris, who seemed to be attached like a magnet to my breast.

I don't think it was just because he was my first-born.

Perhaps the added connection of his birthday being the day after my own gives us this mutual understanding. I can feel his moods, sympathise with his pain, anger and frustration – much linked with his inability to communicate when he was little. We are Geminis together, and it is imperative that we communicate in between seeking our own quiet at the drop of a hat. We are both determined to play and not stop until exhaustion grabs us for necessary sleep, the only device to prevent our enraged tears in case the party goes on without us and we miss something.

I would read Paris to sleep each night cradled in my arms – poems, novels, words against the swelling background of Debussy's 'La Mer', his favourite music for pulling him into the lap of quiet. A slow, solid, immovable sleep.

In my painting studio during the day, he would sit bouncing in his chair or crawling around his playpen for sometimes as long as ten minutes before screaming to be let out. He wasn't an animal to be caged or restrained. I should have known that. Once out, he would happily crawl among my paints and canvases, opening every cupboard in his curiosity. Frequently I would swab the oil paint from his squelching fingers at the end of a day, only to find I was wiping away the colour and joy from his small face.

My life changed for ever with the challenge of entertaining Paris. I learnt to drive in order to get him from baby jungles to biffing activities, playgrounds to swimming-pools, anything to exhaust his endless energy. I pushed him around from one gallery to another, a compromise to be out of the house, but he was never content to be sitting in a pushchair. I would carry him around, explaining to him every painting and sculpture in the Tate and the National Gallery, trying to be oblivious of the queer looks of strangers. Most trips were planned around playgrounds because Paris needed to work off his physical frustration.

I found a child-minder to allow me some time to myself and get back to work, but all I could paint was his picture, dual portraits, Madonna and child. He held his power effortlessly. I was exhausted much of the time. My mother had never told me that this was what having a baby boy was like. How could she? She only had girls, and we were placid twinkling dolls in her memory.

'Boys are different,' she said.

'I know,' I replied.

Sometimes Paris consumed me, all my attention, imagination and strength, until at the end of the day I collapsed into bed like an empty crumpled carton. But the pride I felt that he was my son was a blanket cover of exemption.

My partner was working hard at the time to keep our home warm and paid-for – a young dad's prerogative – so much of the time it was just Paris and me. Our bond was a diamond rope, but his pure vigour and reckless physicality still amazed me. He was a cliché of a boy, striped through like Brighton Rock with his blond, blue-eyed, bully-boy beefiness.

I could no longer imagine how it was before he arrived, with his easy, cherubic grin and his grim, determined pout, any more than I could forget my own physical pain on his arrival. The thought of having more than Paris, or another Paris, left me shell-shocked.

'Go through that again? You must be joking!" I replied to

Alastair's mild enquiry. But the seed was planted in my mind. Every time I looked at Paris I thought how selfish I was being, to leave him as an only child. I could have been happy, but he would never have experienced that rounding, invigorating challenge of sibling rivalry. The daily rows over breakfast, ability, taste, toys and television that unite brothers and sisters world-wide, and make you instantly connect with other first-borns or youngests in other families.

Carson arrived, a girl. It was an immaculate drug- and pain-free birth, which I'd forgotten by the next day. Paris was almost three years old, and both intrigued and cross at having to encompass a sister in his life. Delight mixed with envy as he became the older, grown-up brother who could fetch nappies for the incapable, gurgling sister. Then jealousy would creep out of its wretched corner and I would notice tearful eyes brimming as he watched me change her.

'What's up sweetheart?' I'd ask, hands and attention still engrossed in nappy mess, and he'd say, 'I'm still little too. Why can't I wear nappies and have a dummy?' and I would put a happily unprotesting Carson down. Cuddling and kissing his galumphing limbs, I'd say, 'I know and I love you'; and I would have that conversation that I still haven't finished having with him now he's nine, that goes:

'Paris, you know you will always be the most special boy to me because you were my first baby and you are a boy and I didn't know how to be with you and I've had to learn, as you have to learn how to be with Carson. She will always be your sister, as I will always be your mama, who loves you more than anything in all the world.'

I wonder when I will stop saying this love affirmation, and

hearing Paris reply, 'Tell me again how it was when I was a baby.'

When things started to go wrong between his father and me, Paris was angry and upset a lot of the time. Nothing seemed to placate him. He would fuel our grown-up arguments with his wildly incoherent behaviour. He was sensing our relationship's disorder before we even knew it, a barometer of our troubles that we took no time to read, only our energy to reprimand. He became the difficult child to his little sister's quiet placid twinkling. She was a little dolly, daily dressed in frills, with a dummy in her mouth that Paris would steal and hide, admitting nothing but annoyance at her distress. He strode around the house in Spain to which we had moved, manfully armed to the hilt with every weapon available from his toy box, predictably dressed in one of his uniforms, Batman, Spiderman, Superman, shod in red welly-boots, a sun-bleached crew-cut glowing on top of his bronzed skin, and a sword always at hand. An aggressor's aggressor. Angry tears raced down his accused cheeks at every unfair decision, even if it was only not allowing him a chocolate before lunch. 'It's not fair, you love Carson more than me!' was his endless retort.

Have I made it up or do I remember one of us replying, 'Yes we do, when you behave like this! It's time, young man, you started to grow up!'

And I watched his face crumble white with the weight of his pain and hurt.

He was only little.

It hit me suddenly like a splash of cold water. Paris was in trouble. I was hurting my son and expecting him to be brave and grown-up. For chrissakes, he was only five years old. How much of a man could he be? Why should his shoulders be broad enough to carry the weight of our distress, just because he wore a Superman cape? We had taken him from England, away from his friends, and promised him a land of sun and sea that he didn't want, with a new language to learn. We had placed him in the middle of our personal war zone.

I was unconsciously repeating my own family patterns.

No wonder he started eating for comfort, and developing allergic reactions to everything he wanted most in his mouth. Certain foods made his mood-swings unpredictably bad. He couldn't eat one banana, he had to eat five. Swordfish and tuna, his favourites, cheese, butter, milk, sugar, caffeine and chocolate, all swung him in the wrong direction, as I was told by the Spanish iridologist from whom I sought help. I could see, once I'd been told how it was the wider view, that his small body couldn't take it. Feeding him any of these foods triggered a reaction that he had no control over. It was like lighting the blue touch-paper; even he wanted to stand well back, and he'd watch himself reel out of control, none of us able to find the stop button.

I put him on a strict diet, off all the foods he loved. Things got worse before they got better. His father, Alastair, and I separated. I got on a plane with Paris and Carson and came back to live with my mother for our first year back in London.

At first I took Paris to the paediatric food and allergy unit in Charing Cross Hospital every week. They said that his stomach was over-producing acid, and was irritated by the wrong food. If left unchecked, this would soon produce an ulcer. All acid foods were off, too, until his stomach got its balance back. Then other things could slowly be reintroduced, but nothing in excess – sensible advice for anyone. It frightened me into being conscious not only of what he ate but of what he took in from the rest of the world. I decided there must be no more shouting or rows, and 'Shut up' was banned from the house.

I had found Paris a lovely school, but he found it hard adjusting from the roughness of his Spanish school, which had taught him how to fight like an unruly gladiator and left him confused by an alphabet that sounded different. He wanted nothing more to do with anything from Spain. He said he never wanted to speak the language again. I didn't blame him. Our Spanish year had hit us all hard.

Paris was still angry. He said he wanted to be a judo fighter, and played out endless martial-arts scenarios with his plastic superhuman figures of turtles and Thundercats inside complex Lego installations. He wasn't interested in learning how to read. He studied cartoons tirelessly on TV, repeatedly drawing his favourite characters of play-violence with all the dedication of a Disney storyboarder. He was overtly talented for his age, but didn't want to tie his own laces. In judo classes he worshipped his teacher and threw himself into unleashing his energy, determined to win each round, never giving up and almost always succeeding. At school his teacher said he was stupid and a bully, a disruption to the class who fell into wars with the other 'difficult' children. He failed all the first school curriculum tests and they suggested extra tuition. How they could not see that this child was brilliant was beyond me. I had to practise patience and keep the faith.

All this time I was mending myself from the break-up of my nine-year relationship and trying to establish another way of being myself, as was his Dad, back in England and seeing the kids. But I was always certain of Paris winning through. No matter what anybody said, he remained in my eyes a clever, beautiful boy and, most importantly, always kind to others if not to himself. I knew that like me he just needed time to show the rest of the world he was a swan. As Alastair and I recovered ourselves, Paris and Carson were like shining reflections of our new, brighter selves.

One day it happened. I was called in by his new teacher and asked what was happening. Suddenly Paris was doing everything, capable of anything. I smiled, unsurprised. For a moment I wanted to say, like some juvenile, 'Told you so!'

Now, glowing with academic achievements and friendships he has discovered sport, packing away his toys in favour of sporting equipment. I, chief football-hater, now sit down to watch matches with him as he explains the politics and skill-tactics attached to every game, and the chance of Man United winning the European Cup without including him in the team. He no longer wants to be a cartoonist but centre forward for Manchester United during the winter and Wimbledon tennis champion during the summer, now he's been picked out for squad training by the Lawn Tennis Association.

'I don't see why not. Just because Aggassi and Becker don't play for Arsenal and Cantona didn't win the French Open, that doesn't mean it's not possible,' I counsel.

Because of Paris, I have become something I never thought I'd be, a chauffeur mum. Relaying car-loads of muddy, smutty boys to matches, games and challenges, I turn deaf ears to their swearing and giggles, and try to keep a straight face at their pre-pubescent talk of snogging, sex and 'it', which keeps them roaring for hours.

Already, I have seen Paris, at eight, through the first traumas of lovesickness. A crush on a beautiful girl in his class had him wobbling for weeks at every wiggle of her little finger, every bat of a lash, as she cruelly played him off against his friends for her demanding royal attention.

Strange feelings released themselves into my bloodstream. In playground fights I had often wanted to take up arms and win his battles, but I knew I must keep back so that the triumph could be his. But this love thing was different. I wanted to throw this eight-year-old hussy against a wall and tattoo her with 'HARLOT' for infecting my son with her smiles, for stringing him along on some muddy-bumpy hay-ride that he's never signed up for. He was too young to be describing those familiar pains in his chest that I knew weren't indigestion (not from my cooking, anyway), but nearer to cardiac arrest.

The feelings of a million mothers for a thousand years about their sons, I discovered, were not the sole right of the Jewish or Italian caricature mama (unless my mother hadn't told me the truth about my 'real' father). I was locked in there too. I even heard myself telling him, as if from some hackneyed soap script, 'I wouldn't bother with her, Paris. You've got plenty of years for playing around with girls, just have fun with your friends. Besides, the sad truth is that if you ignore her she's bound to come running. Chase after her, telling her you love her, and she'll run in the opposite direction.'

How many mothers, over the years, have told their sons these tales which reinforce the behaviour to keep us all on this roundabout! But I didn't want him to get hurt. What I meant to say to him was 'Don't give your power away and you won't get hurt.'

I know about girls like these, I've been one.

A friend said the other day: 'The thing is about us boys is that we always love our mothers totally until we fall in love, and then we transfer it all to a woman whom we expect our mothers to love as much as we do.' I gulped in guilt.

'Boys are different,' Paris said to me, riding on the top of the bus the other day.

'Why's that?' I asked.

'Because we need more space than girls. Girls can play in a room together and they always expect boys to want to, but boys need to be able to run around and play before we want to stay in. That's why we have to look tough, to make girls leave us alone.'

Sometimes the simplest explanations for the complications of sexual politics can be found in the playground. Now I know that men will willingly return home when they feel they have enough space, and their toughness is just territorial Teflon – and I wish Paris had been my brother to tell me all this when I was sixteen.

I used to worry about my son growing older and not wanting to hold my hand or give spontaneous cuddles. I heard tales that boys became embarrassed by public shows of affection. I saw it with my stepbrothers and boys in my class, hands always in pockets – the only hands they let touch them were their own. But Paris seems to become more affectionate as he grows older. He demands as just and right nightly bedtime hugs and to sit cosily next to me on the sofa at reading-time. Sometimes Carson falls asleep and we stay up late and watch some so-called unsuitable film, laughing, talking and crying together at the appropriate bits.

I was brought up with no religious knowledge by a proud breed of atheists, but I always held on to a small core of belief that I must have been born with; it certainly wasn't intentionally planted. In both my children I have seeded an understanding of God and of their own spiritual content and connection. That doesn't mean I take them to church every week, and they hated Sunday school. But we do pray together, for others and for ourselves, and give thanks for the joy and gifts we have. Having an understanding with God about the way life can be, I know that everything is in the right place at the right time. I have been given the treasures of children to understand and to learn from about my own disabilities and intolerances, and my inability to tell men from boys. I have come to learn, understand and love the joys of football, or of energy expended as an end in itself, because of Paris being in my life.

Chemical imbalances can still throw his body and mood. One can of Coke and I see in him myself thrown off course by a thoughtless cup of coffee on an empty stomach. His joy becomes mine on Christmas morning or over 'man of the match' achievements. Watching him taking part in life, and succeeding, is better than any Hollywood movie or West End play, even if it is because I am the executive producer having my ego vicariously massaged by my home-grown talent.

These are the things, along with the excessive pain of child-birth, that nobody tells you about, that can't be conveyed, that you're never prepared for. I don't suppose I would have listened anyway. There is no way to be prepared for the overwhelming love for the alien being that is pulled from your womb and dumped, slimy with blood, upon your naked skin, that grows into a cross-cuckoo, plump toddler and then stretches into a skinny, sinewy, sharp-humoured, philosophical youth. Already I catch glimpses of him as an adult. I catch his physical shape as a ghost in crowded streets. Facing me in serious or laughing discussion, his features transmogrify into adult form before melting back.

I look now at young men whom I once desired and bid for before bedding and shedding, and I look at them differently. I admire their handsome, beautifully shaped heads, elegant noses, the way of their eyes, the turn of their mouths, and I am excited by their clever, caring answers to our social and political futures. Most of all, I see my son in them and feel proud. Any other man in my life would have to measure up to Paris's (and Carson's) approval. I can't ever imagine feeling embarrassed by his side, by his appearance or beliefs even when he asks me, 'Mum, aren't you a bit overdressed?'

'No.' I repeat what my mother always told me. 'You can never be overdressed, only under.'

'Yeah, yeah?' he replies cynically, and we both laugh.

I miss not having more time with him alone, as I still have with my daughter while he is off on his sporting triumphs. But she is not so far behind. She is at school now, and soon enough she will have her own agenda.

Working at home, I give priority to my kids, and I choose

not to have a nanny. If I haven't managed to finish my work by the time they come back from school, or back from spending the weekend with their Dad, that is my problem. I can always work once they get to bed. Anyway, I have the rest of my life to work, and we have only the next ten years together playing at home, before I buy him his round-the-world air ticket to broaden his horizons, invent his own possibilities and do his own washing.

As Paris tells his bemused friends, 'You see life is like a game of football, isn't it, Mum? You have to keep the goal in sight, and the best way to score is by sharing the ball, and it's never worth fouling when God is the referee!'

Of all the challenges and successes I have in my life, past and future, I want most in the world to do the right thing as a mother. I want my son to grow up to love and be proud of himself, to know that he is responsible for his own happiness and that he can achieve anything that he sets his heart upon. If he leaves home knowing all this and realises that I will always champion him and love him unconditionally, any other achievement in my life is an acorn to this oak.

God Bless All Our Mothers

MICHAEL SEED

Michael Seed was born in Manchester in 1957. He entered the Franciscan Friars of the Atonement in 1978 and was ordained a Catholic priest in 1986. Since then he has served as a chaplain in Westminster Cathedral and as Ecumenical Officer at Archbishop's House, Westminster.

'To lose one parent, Mr Worthing, may be regarded as a misfortune; to lose both looks like carelessness.' The difficulty was that *I* had lost two *sets* of parents – one being more lost than the other. Having just discovered the works of the late Oscar Wilde at the age of fifteen, it was quite a shock to be called to the headmaster's office and told that my late parents had not been my natural parents at all. All I remember is that I was initially glad that I was not going to be disciplined for anything.

With Oscar's words ringing in my ears, it was difficult to know why my grandmother had not previously said anything to me about this. Perhaps I, like Mr Worthing, JP, had been found at Victoria Station, my Alma Mater, close to which I have had the pleasure, for the last twelve years, of living.

In June 1957, let us say at Victoria Station because I did not actually know where, it was reported that I was born. (I have subsequently found out that it was not at the station but in Manchester.) The session with my headmaster came as a major revelation. My grandmother, who was my legal guardian after the death of my adoptive mother in 1966, was very worried that I would disown her if the truth about my background were revealed. It seems that my natural mother was a very young lady when she bore me, and that there is no record of who my natural father was. I discovered that my real name was Steven Wayne Godwin and not Michael Seed. I have always aspired to be like the characters of the Western movie genre and so it was good to learn that I had at least some connection with the Wild West in my nomenclature.

Leaving the headmaster's office, I started to ask myself, 'Who was my father?' and 'Where is my mother?' – interesting questions, which I recall have some biblical precedents. My grandmother need have had no fear of my disowning her. I realised that all my relatives were indeed adoptive ones. I had always wondered why I did not look like any of them. But I owe the greatest debt to my now late grandmother Mary, who actually raised me like a mother, as I hope to show.

It would seem that I was adopted in 1958 by Joseph and Lillian Seed of Manchester. They adopted me from the Catholic Children's Society of Salford. I am informed that they adopted two babies but sent one back; I have always wondered what became of the other (perhaps he or she is reading this chapter), and why it wasn't me.

My adoptive mother came from strong Salvation Army roots and my father from Catholic stock in Liverpool. As you can see, my religious schizophrenia started at a tender age. My earliest recollections of life at home with my mother are happy ones; we lived in a cake-shop and sold confectionery. What child would not be happy? My father went out to work each day to Strangeways Prison as a warder. It was through his work that I developed my love of millinery, I think – police and firemen's helmets, as well as his warder's cap, were regular features of life, as members of all these professions were regular visitors and customers of the shop. But this idyllic childhood was soon to be shattered.

My earliest recollection of a problem was that my mother always seemed very distant, though not in her expression of love for me. It was only subsequently that I learnt she was addicted to heavy tranquillizers. I remember at about four or five years old being pushed, with my mother, into the fire-place (it was not lit at the time) by my father; he was at times angry at her for her inability to cope without this medication. On reflection, his anger, and my mother's addiction, might have been due to their inability to have children of their own. I do, however, remember a happy fifth birthday party.

Our little confectionary shop had to be demolished in the wake of massive redevelopment of a very deprived area of Manchester; the development included the major supermarkets. This made us homeless and impecunious, and both my parents were at this time unemployed. We moved to live with my adoptive mother's mother in Bolton. Little did I think that things could go from bad to worse, but they did. Within eighteen months of our arrival in Bolton my dear mother was dead.

It was a Saturday morning like any other for a child of eight. I was preparing for Saturday-morning cinema where my grandfather was an usher, though I only remember him as the lollipop man. I was playing in the kitchen on my typewriter – many say I have not stopped playing on such machines since – when there was a knock at the door. My grandmother opened the door. 'It's Lillian,' a neighbour said. 'Come quickly!'

I was never to discover the full horror of her tragic end. It seems that my mother had placed herself on the local branch line of the railway, a railway I had to cross each day on the way to school. From that day onwards I became a recluse. I wanted nothing to do with anyone. I never played with my child's typewriter again. Schooling became too painful, and from the age of eight until I was sixteen, the years were years of child psychiatrists, social workers and, later, a special school in Rochdale for what were then known as 'maladjusted children'.

Within less than two years both my father and grandfather were dead. Shortly after my mother's death, my father developed a tumour on the brain and I did not see him in the year preceding his death. He had taken me to Liverpool to live with his parents following my mother's death, to get me away from the tragic environment. This was just before he fell ill. However, before he was permanently hospitalised, he took me back to my grandmother in Bolton, as this was where I had some roots; indeed, my grandmother was missing me. She was in a state of shock and bereavement herself: she had lost her daughter and her husband within a short time, as well as the young life in the house.

I returned to my primary school in Bolton, once again having to cross the tragic railway bridge. Most of the children were wonderful, but some made my life unbearable, mocking and jeering. I was a totally withdrawn student, failing all examinations. The headmaster had to give me private tuition in reading and writing, and I did not learn either of those skills until the age of eleven. Failing my 'eleven plus', I was sent to a secondary modern school, where I was unable to keep my life together. Social workers intervened and I was invited to go and see a brand-new school in Rochdale which I have already mentioned. I should have said that on hearing of my father's death (on returning home from my primary school) from my grandmother at the gate of the house, I swore an oath that I would take my life at the age of thirteen. Thus, aged twelve, I felt that it did not really matter anyway where I lived. I was not able to make any rational decisions, so my life would take a new turn whatever was to happen.

My grandmother missed me greatly when I was in Rochdale, as I could only visit her for one weekend a month. I had to agree to leave home as my grandmother, by this point, was almost eighty and simply unable to cope, physically or mentally, with a young brat. My thirteenth birthday came, and I was enjoying my new life in Rochdale so much that I had forgotten that I should actually be dead. So I decided that I would take a new oath, that I would live to sixteen – what had I to lose?

Why was the school a happy place? Because of the arrival of a certain teacher, a very special teacher. He started to develop a very deep care for me. He was an Anglican priest who had decided he needed to take a break from parochial responsibilities and use his educational skills. This teacher was a breath of fresh air, as all the other teachers seemed only intent on training us for the factory jobs which were all they felt that any of us was capable of. I had decided to become, along with my grandmother, a strict and particular Baptist. My friend (as he became) smoked and drank and was very, very high-church, so high-church that he even crocheted his own vestments for 'Mass' (something I knew little about at this time); I, of course, in my puritan state, was horrified by his behaviour! However, he insisted on talking to me about the Catholic faith, proponents of which I sincerely believed would not be going anywhere near heaven.

Later on, I went to my teacher-friend and told him that I was so confused about this religion lark that I would like to take a sabbatical and become a temporary atheist. He laughed. As we did no studies towards formal examinations, we were comparatively free to occupy our time as we pleased. My teacher set me the works of Marx, Hegel, Nietzsche and, for bedtime reading, as a special treat, *Mein Kampf* and *The Origin of Species*. After a year of this, I ran back to Christianity with great haste; my teacher was pleasantly pleased. I began to ask myself how anyone could be such a universal man as he was and how I could emulate him. He seemed like yet another mother to me, and one whom I could admire, respect and love. He constantly challenged me with his wisdom and willed me to do well.

So at the age of fourteen my horizons at last seemed to be broadening. By this point I was allowed home to my grandmother every weekend. She was always so happy for every moment that we were together. I had always admired her

faith: every morning and night she would say prayers. As a little child I would continue to watch the television while she
said her prayers. The sound of her favourite Christian ditties
was always on her lips; it was wonderful to be watching *Dr
Who?* while in the background my grandmother would be
singing 'Onward Christian Soldiers' or 'Oh! for a closer walk
with God.' She had never doubted the existence of God. I
had. It was at this time, during these regular weekend visits,
that I became more and more involved in our Baptist church.
I met there a student for the Baptist ministry and he invited
me to visit his Bible college. I felt that I should be baptised,
which in the Baptist tradition enables one to enter into full
membership of the Church. It was discovered that I had
already been 'done' as a little baby by my natural mother,
before she placed me with the Catholic Children's Society. So
with two baptisms, I then considered 'the call' to the Baptist
ministry – my first thoughts of vocation.

However, my teacher-friend and his influence gave me a
nagging feeling that I ought to consider his tradition of ministry also. I began to think back to my early years at Catholic
primary schools. But for an Independent Baptist, Catholics
were considered 'beyond the pale', a view I have yet to reflect
upon. I invited my teacher-friend to my second baptism,
which took place in a very cold Baptist church in Farnworth
in a district called Moses' Gate; Moses, I believe, has much to
do with water, though the water in the tank for my baptism
was freezing, most unlike that of the Red Sea. The minister
who was to perform the ceremony appeared in liturgical
green waders (a practice that Westminster Cathedral has yet to
adopt), and proceeded to hear my personal testimony of faith

before my immersion in the tank. At this point, I recalled a little more of my reading of Mr Wilde. I believe it was Dr Chasuble who stated that 'Sprinkling is all that is necessary, or indeed I think advisable.' Given the coldness of the water, I wholeheartedly agreed with him. It was, however, on my third immersion that I became convinced that the Almighty had remembered my oath at the age of thirteen and intended to take me to His Kingdom there and then, albeit a few months short of my sixteenth birthday. One of the great sayings of my grandmother was, 'It is better to live a bit longer in this world than be too soon in the next.' I wasn't sure at the age of thirteen, when I made my oath, that I agreed with her.

There are so many funny and loving memories of my relationship with my grandmother, one of which is our journeying to an evangelistic rally in Manchester. Our driver was my rather eccentric Aunt Dorothy, who was known to pray with her eyes closed while driving: hence my grandmother's remark, previously quoted. Another amusing memory is of my grandmother's wisdom concerning public transport on cold Sunday evenings. It used to take us two bus rides from home to the Salvation Army Citadel in Bolton, but only one bus ride to the strict and particular Baptist church. It was for this reason that our allegiance shifted, though I do not recommend such considerations as a way of discerning where to find God in your life. We discovered the Baptist church which was to become our spiritual home through an 'uncle' (who, although a Baptist minister, claimed not to believe in baptism), a travelling evangelist who was preaching at this church in Bolton. I hope that my description of myself as a religious schizophrenic is now making some sense.

My sense of religious vocation had many shortcomings. I started to wonder if it was all a 'running away', a 'leaving the world'. I was very, very frightened of leaving school, a place where I had found stability, security and love. Was I prepared to be an adult, or even a frightened child, in such a big world without the support of a 'mother'? How could I talk to my grandmother about my fears, aspirations and concerns, especially as I developed my own self-awareness? I know that I would have been embarrassed to share some of my inmost thoughts with her, given that she was of such advanced years. I must have made her life difficult, despite the joy of our meetings on my weekend visits, particularly in my teens. I was always awkward (who wouldn't be, given my history?) and slightly angry, frustrated and withdrawn.

One must remember the label given me by the school, 'maladjusted' – a word I have learnt to hate, for it imposes limitations not of one's own choosing. It is a word that concludes; it does not enable. I was grateful for the opportunity of taking an O level in art, a subject I love, at a local comprehensive school in Rochdale. I was always considered the boy from the school for 'strange kids' and that had its effect – I started to believe it. Some of the pupils were mocking, yet others were sensitive, much as is always the case in life. However, I found my weekly visits had a profound effect on how I was learning to cope with the idea of leaving school. I am very proud of the fact, given all that had happened in my formative years, that I was the first student to take any exams from my 'special' school and, indeed, I left school with two O levels, in art and English.

As I neared the age of sixteen, my departure from the security of school drew closer and closer – too close, in fact, for comfort. What would I do with my life and would I ever feel wanted, needed or, indeed, loved? I came to the conclusion that one had to 'shut up and put up', an understanding it has taken me a long while to put into practice.

So, it was 1974 and I was to leave my school. I returned once again to live with my grandmother in Bolton. I had to find some gainful employment and at the age of sixteen, with few qualifications and, as I thought, no hope, the search was more than fraught. I read an advertisement in the *Bolton Evening News*: help was needed in a motorway café. My grandmother thought that I should 'go for it' and, let's face it, what had I to lose? Sadly, I was sacked within a little while, two days in fact. I had broken numerous trays of eggs, smashed trolley-loads of crockery and I felt that I needed a strong gin – not that I was drinking at that stage, as I remained a strict and particular Baptist, but was this a foretaste of my life to come? I found it very difficult and very frightening to earn a living, or even to acknowledge that I had to. And all this time, all I could ask was, where was my mother? She would have known how to cope – maybe.

A serious depression descended. I had not made a success of this attempt, and I no longer had the support network of psychiatrists and social workers that had regulated so much of my life over the last four years. I could not share my deepest feelings and fears with anyone, let alone myself or my grand-mother. I used to get angry with her, and yet I was really angry with my mother for not being there, and then angry with myself for being angry, and so it went on. I needed to be loved (and to feel it) and also to be able to give love (and feel that it was being received).

My second job (just to lift the gloom a bit for the reader) was in a rather posh menswear shop. This lasted slightly longer than my previous attempt, but after three weeks they too had had enough. I had managed to blow up the kitchen. It has to be admitted that I had never up to this point made, let alone drunk, a cup of tea or coffee. I had no idea how to make these eccentric beverages; my grandmother had never tasted a cup of tea in her life, as she drank only orange juice and milk (a substance I have not touched since my early years, following a bad experience in the confectionary shop where I guzzled a bottle of sour milk). I placed the electric kettle, with lead and plug, in the gas oven, with disastrous consequences. I had further been reprimanded by the manager for sending customers to shops where they might be able to purchase the same items at much less cost. Was this also, perhaps, a sign of things to come?

My grandmother was, understandably, becoming more and more distressed. I saw an advertisement for a care assistant in a hostel for the elderly and mentally ill (where I felt that I myself should have been a patient, as I felt like a sixteen-year-old with the cares of an eighty-year-old). It was with the same social service department with which I was still 'in care' (and was to remain so until the age of eighteen). I attended an interview at the home and, by some chance, was accepted by the husband and wife who were responsible for its running. This couple had children of my age and I think that they took pity on me, for I was instantly accepted as a member of their family. I was so happy, having at last found some of the peace and space that I had been longing for. I started to socialise with their children and even attended a number of dances – not that I have ever mastered the skill of dancing, but I was at least mixing in 'normal' circumstances with my contemporaries. I felt accepted. I did not have to explain. This was a most unusual feeling. They had seen me for who I was, not as the person I thought I should be nor as a person who had to please and to *earn* love.

I became a responsible person in the home and felt at last that I was being taken seriously. It was at this time that one of our residents, a wonderfully dressed rag-and-bone man, brought home a brand-new copy of the 1974 *Salford Catholic Directory*. I knew little about Roman Catholics except that they were all damned. This directory was placed in my hands, much to my dismay, that evening at supper. The rag-and-bone man was so distressed by the delay in the arrival of his supper owing to my reading of this volume that he consumed the home's pet goldfish on toast – much to my horror, as even at this stage I had an affinity with animals that would eventually lead to my becoming a Franciscan.

I tried to share my religious feelings at this time with my grandmother. It was, as you may imagine, very difficult because she was wholly set in her understanding. I reflected on the faith of my parents and considered what my current faith might mean to them, and how they might, if they were here, help me to determine my own faith-journey now. One evening, instead of joining my grandmother for the service at the Baptist church, I decided to cross the street and attend a Church of England service to find out exactly what went on there and what it was that my teacher-friend had so enthused about.

The vicar at this church was not as I had expected. My

only experience of Church of England priests was my teacher-friend, and so when I encountered the evangelical wing of the Church of England, I was not moved as I had hoped to be. I felt a calling to a community life, and I had heard of various religious orders in the Church of England. The Anglican vicar (with whom I spoke) did not share this interest and I was most disappointed. I spoke to a friend of mine whose sympathies lay with the more 'high-church' understanding of the Church of England, and he suggested that I might look towards the Roman Catholic Church. I had, however, promised the evangelical Church of England vicar that I would be 'received' into his Church; I was received during Evensong and remained an Anglican for the winter.

These events helped me on a universal spiritual pilgrimage which for some reason, unbeknown to me at the time, led me to explore the idea of entering into communion with the Roman Catholic Church. It was with some fear that I attended a Sunday-night Mass in a Catholic church over the road from the Anglican church where I had sought a home. (It was opposite a public house which I believed to be very sinful.) The congregation of the Mass was mixed: half was drunk, the other half was saying the rosary. The smell, a mingling of incense (which I had never encountered before) and alcohol, and the sight of many people on their knees fiddling with odd beads, were most moving. *This* was a Church for sinners, I thought. I somehow knew that Our Lord was present, despite the overriding smell of alcohol. I have since learnt from many Christmases at the cathedral that we are more likely (as George Herbert suggests) to find Our Lord among the 'down and outs' and drunkards than in the temples and courts.

What an image! How could I do anything but ring the doorbell of the parish priest? I remember that he was very elderly and most surprised that I, a stranger, should ring his bell, especially on a Sunday night, asking to become a Catholic. I have reflected on this many times since, and thought that Our Lord does seem to call at the most inconvenient and unexpected times! The priest opened the door to me with a certain understandable caution, and I tried to explain the contents of this chapter in a few minutes – I was still on the doorstep at this point. He invited me in (why do priests always seem to take so long to do this?) and offered me a drink – a drink! a drink! is this man serious? To my astonishment he told me that I was already a Catholic – one of those, you'll remember, doomed to go straight to nowhere – and that I needed a few little chats and a good confession. Well, I had never heard of a confession.

I went home happy, yet I guess perplexed and sad; how on earth could I explain *this* one to my grandmother? I also felt a calling to the priesthood, a calling that I had somehow known existed under and within my calling to the Baptist ministry; yet I had not even understood, let alone experienced, the sacrament of penance, let alone any of the other truths of the Catholic faith. I did share with my grandmother my re-discovered faith (not as she might have hoped, of course). She was shocked, but received my news with respect. I had not believed that anyone could respect that I had made a conscious decision of my own, and that the decision too would be respected: it was strange. This was, of course, the love of a 'mother' for her son on first hearing news of his independence. I have certainly treasured that moment ever since.

Looking in my new *Salford Directory*, I confused the telephone number of the priest responsible for vocations with that of the missionary director of the diocese. I dialled the number and spoke to the director who, of course, assumed that I had a vocation to be a priest in the nether regions of the earth (as the psalmist might put it). I found myself – probably against my better judgement, but God *does* work in a mysterious way – having an interview with the Society of African Missions. I took this as God's will. It was God's will until I was twenty-one, when I understood that He had been trying to tell me (no doubt, shouting at me) that I should get out and find a different vocation, in a community where my history and background would be understood and treasured.

So where does this leave me? I had experienced in my short time many varied and differing emotional, physical and spiritual worlds with many differing models of stability. I knew that I still missed my mother and had searched diligently for a substitute. While the love of mother and son can never truly be replaced, I did find that those who entered my life came very near and ended up meaning in some ways far more: my grandmother, that rock who, though sceptical of my 'vocation' to that Church of people who would 'go nowhere fast', understood her own calling to the Lord's kingdom as a Catholic at the age of ninety; the teacher-friend who, though he remains in a different communion, did so much to bring me to the position of joy in which I now find myself; and, of course, my own natural mother, without whom I would not be here and for whom I can only pray. I did actually try to find her through the Salford Catholic Children's Society, and I had the fortune to meet Sister Philomena, with whom both my adoptive and natural mothers had dealt: what a joy it was to meet such a figure after some seventeen years. The 'unknown' about my natural mother was eased – a little. There is also my dear adoptive mother who, though she ultimately could not see a way to resolving her life, gave me so much joy and happiness in the brief years that I knew her. However, the one person without mention of whom this article would remain incomplete is, of course, that mother who remained with me (little did I know it) throughout this period – Our Lady, the Blessed Virgin Mary.

It is difficult for some to see how a Jewish woman who appears as a vulnerable, insecure vessel in her early teens can become that icon, that beacon of hope and of womanhood, for so many saints and sinners. To have been there for me, for each one of us, is such a mystery of paradox. She was, and she is, that juxtaposition of divinity and humanity for which we all, saints and sinners, believers and non-believers, search. She gave herself freely; she said 'Yes'. That is all that any of us can do. She, despite the awful nature of life, the horrors that are thrown at us, still remains that beacon, that selfless hope, for each of us and for all eternity. If only all our stories could be such a model of love and giving *without* the pain, how easy it would be! But, and here's the rub, it isn't like that. Yet we know, even if we are not aware of it, that She, Our Lady, is there, comforting, holding and loving us through all the horrors of life, and that it is with Her that we can truly say 'thy kingdom come'.

For those of you who find this religion lark too much (and you may call me, as I have called myself, a religious schizophrenic), perhaps these words from *A Woman of No Importance* will serve to show how my life has been: 'The Book of Life begins with a man and a woman in a garden.' To which comes the reply: 'It ends with Revelations.' God bless all our mothers, those of whom we are directly aware and those who may not appear so directly: those who structure and those who sustain and those, for each of us, who offer life to one another.

Casting Off

Sonia Melchett

Sonia Melchett is the author of three books: Tell Me, Honestly, Someone is Missing: a Memoir *and* Passionate Quests. *She has three children and is married to the writer Andrew Sinclair.*

Peter was not meant to have been born at all – or so the gynaecologist tried to convince me when I was two months pregnant. Julian Mond, my first husband, and I had been married just over two months, so Peter must have been conceived in a small hotel in Leno, on the banks of Lake Como, where we spent our honeymoon. I was ill most of the time with what the Italian doctor dismissed as 'honeymoon sickness'. Returning to London we had to find somewhere to live. I trailed around various depressing areas looking for a flat we could afford, but ended up in a charming tiny mews house which we most certainly couldn't afford.

In the meantime Julian, just out of the Fleet Air Arm, was earning a living by flying cargoes of cattle to Germany in old transport planes. We had married young – I was twenty and Julian twenty-one – not a popular move with his parents,

Lord and Lady Melchett, who refused us any financial support. In spite of this, it should have been a blissful time but for the fact that, having found somewhere to live, I immediately became sick again and was threatening to miscarry. The gynaecologist warned me that unless I stayed in bed for at least five months, I would probably lose the baby altogether, and he suggested I have a *dilatation et curettage* and think of starting a family when we were more settled.

There was no question in my mind that I wanted this particular child, and so I took to my bed while my poor husband had to manage his job, furnish the house with the bare essentials and cope with the domesticities of life. It was a strange period. From my bed I gazed through the window at the comings and goings of the various householders round the courtyard of the mews, weaving tales about them which turned out to be even less enthralling than the characters we later met.

While lying there Peter was turning somersaults inside me which ended six months later in a 'breech birth', which the gynaecologist performed with great skill in our small bedroom, not helped by my somewhat hysterical mother, in tears and brandishing a glass of whisky. In between the whiffs of pentathol, the pain was excruciating, and at one point I'm convinced I had an 'after life' experience when I was travelling down a long tunnel with a light at the end which I nearly reached. However, with the aid of forceps, the present Peter Melchett, executive director of Greenpeace UK, saw the light of day bawling his head off. Having no cot, he spent his first weeks in a drawer and started to grow into a beautiful, though not exactly robust, baby with a mass of blond curls. In fact, it became a source of constant embarrassment to me when I wheeled him in his pram round Hyde Park to be endlessly stopped by doting ladies saying, 'What a beautiful little girl you have.' I had immediately regained my health and was now able to 'pull my weight' (my mother's favourite phrase) in our marriage.

Julian had decided to leave Air Contractors, and started a company called British Field Products. He firmly believed that England should become self-supporting in animal feed – he had taken a course in agriculture while in the navy and was encouraged by a family friend, Sir Solly Zuckerman. So, with the self-confidence and optimism of youth and a grant from the government, he set up the company on a disused airfield in Norfolk. The hangars were his office and the control tower our home. Julian worked a twelve-hour day, renting land from Norfolk farmers and producing nasty-looking little pellets of animal food processed in a machine he had bought from Germany. It was a strange and lonely life for Peter and me, who were left to our own devices.

For the first two years we had no car and, apart from the occasional expedition to Blakeney beach with kind friends, we spent our time in the control tower or in the surrounding fields. I don't think I was a particularly good mother. I remember worrying incessantly about how little food Peter seemed to need, and used to try everything to encourage him to stay sitting in his high chair until he had finished his mashed vegetables, which usually ended up being thrown on to the wooden floorboards. Nowadays, I see my children being eminently sensible with their own young, having read all the right manuals on child-care.

After a few years, with the success of the company our fortunes improved and we moved to a rented cottage at Burnham Ovary Steithe which looked over wild marshland with nothing between us and the North Pole. It was a favourite spot for artists and Edward Seago, Pete's godfather, would often stay; he painted some of his best work there.

Perhaps Pete subconsciously absorbed some of this wild atmosphere and the constant bird life passing by which was later to be so important to him. When my daughter, Kerena, was born a year later, we rented a house in the grounds of Holkham Hall and life became slightly more conventional. A series of nannies came and left – I must have been a bad picker. One was a charming old Irish lady who had a habit of chain-smoking and dropping ash over the children's cots; another was a young Norland-trained nymphomaniac who kept open house to a stream of Norfolk youths, and a third an extremely strict suppressed spinster who tried to turn the children into Edwardian paragons of virtue.

In the meantime Julian's career was changing. A new government had reversed the agricultural policy and decided that importing animal feed from abroad made better economic sense. A government official was appointed to oversee the gradual winding down of the company, which became virtually bankrupt. Luckily Samuels, a city merchant bank that had invested in it, backed Julian and invited him to join their board. This meant he had to spend nearly all his time in London at the bank, and Pete became my closest confidant. In retrospect I suppose I treated him too much like an adult, sharing with him some of my present fears and problems and my future dreams. It was an intimate relationship, and perhaps a burden for a young and sensitive boy, but as I was only in my late twenties at the time it seemed completely natural.

The two children and I found ourselves living between the London mews house, which we had repossessed, and yet another rented house in Norfolk, this time at Blakeney, with a garden adjoining the graveyard of the old church. I had by now learnt to drive and loved speeding up to London in my car with the children bouncing about in the back – no seat-belts then.

When the time approached for Pete to leave home and go to prep school – a custom I now believe to be barbaric – I visited about eight of the schools with the best reputations both for education and humanity. Each seemed more Dickensian than the last. Eventually I settled on one on the south coast of Kent where they had a separate house for the first-year boys, apart from the main school, and where the eight-year-olds would be allowed luxuries such as bringing their own cuddly toys and pet rabbits. It seemed a civilised arrangement, but Pete later told me that more bullying went on there than at any other time in his school career. However, on the occasional days out, when Julian and I would drive him to some depressing seaside hotel to lunch in a large, draughty dining-room, he gave no hint of what he was going through.

I remember these outings as extremely uneasy occasions of false cheerfulness and stilted conversation, with no distractions except walks along a pebbly beach. I could sense that Pete wasn't happy, but I thought hopefully that he would soon settle down and make friends. He always insisted that everything was fine and tried to entertain us with anecdotes about the eccentricities of certain masters. But the most lingering memory I have is of waving goodbye from the car window to a thin, pale-faced boy in overlarge grey shorts waiting in the drive until we were out of sight.

When Pete was nearly eleven, we at last found a country home of our own. It was a derelict farmstead near Hunstanton with around eight hundred acres of stony land which the experts told us would never do well. How wrong they were. While we were restoring the old farmhouse, we lived in a caravan parked in a field which a few years later we turned into a tennis court. That same year we bought some land on a steep cliff at Formentor in Majorca overlooking a private bay and started building a small villa. I also became pregnant with my third child, Pandora, and at the same time started writing my first novel. It was certainly a productive year.

After Pandora's birth I spent more and more time travelling with my husband on business trips abroad during the elder children's term-time. But holidays were sacrosanct and were spent either in Majorca or at the farm. As our fortunes improved with Julian's success as a merchant banker, he bought a Cessna aircraft and would fly himself down at weekends, landing in a field near the house. Our humdrum life would become a whirl of activity – long riding expeditions down the Peddars Way, gallops along the sandy beaches, shooting house-parties with a catholic mixture of guests from the worlds of politics, business and the local farming community. Pete would throw himself into everything and was quite capable of having heated arguments with a government minister or a local magistrate at dinners which lasted late into the night. Later he gave up blood sports and took to bird-watching instead, but at the time he was a very good shot.

Soon summer holidays were spent abroad, and friends of all ages and assorted political beliefs descended on the villa. When his father was called away, which often happened, Pete would take his place as host quite effortlessly. He and I had an innate understanding of each other's needs and, I think, we still have. Whether sexuality is a part of this relationship, only Freudians would know.

One August the family was alone in the villa with only Pete's friend Patrick Wedd and his sister Cassandra as guests. Patrick had film-star looks and Cassandra had the face of a Madonna, but they were both painfully shy. It didn't help that Kerena immediately fell for Patrick, and there was certainly no lack of attraction between his sister and Pete. My husband, who would normally have lightened the atmosphere, was ill in bed with mumps, and I found things decidedly sticky. I decided to lay on a trip to the port in our speedboat and a visit to the local disco. After a jolly dinner, while casting off the mooring rope of the boat I lost my balance and fell into the stinking water wearing my best Gucci pants. This episode at least broke the ice.

At the end of one summer holiday Pete and I drove back to London in my open sports car and were in a particularly light-hearted mood. As we sped north along the Route du Sol, singing at the tops of our voices, we realised it was getting dark and we hadn't booked rooms for the night. I wasn't particularly worried, but after being turned away from at least a dozen hotels, we eventually found a rather seedy establishment where we were offered a room. I thought the large jewelled lady behind the desk looked at Pete a little dubiously, but it wasn't until the next morning that we realised we'd spent the night in a brothel – a fact Pete was later able to boast about at school.

As my younger daughter, Pandora, grew up, Pete virtually took over her education. She was a mischievous child with an enormous curiosity and he, with infinite patience, would reply in detail to all her questions, in spite of the fact that his answers were often way above her head. I thought at the time that he would, in fact, have made a very good teacher.

I suppose the first real turning-point in our relationship was when he went to Eton. He was convinced he only passed the entrance exam because (he believed) his prep schoolmaster had opened the question papers the night before and lectured the boys on a particular period of history not previously covered in their curriculum. But pass he did, into the house of our choice, run by a charming and rather vague man whose only real passions were rowing and music.

The prefects who ran the school were a law unto themselves and a few used their powers unmercifully, picking on the prettiest boys to do their fagging for them. This sometimes consisted of sending obscene notes to boys in other houses. Pete still looked slightly effeminate, although he was as strong as an ox and a demon at rowing. It was not done to make a fuss about what was normal practice at the time, but when this happened to Pete he had the courage to step out of line and protested to the house-master, who immediately took drastic action.

I knew nothing until much later about the bullying that went on, yet once again I was aware that when I took him out on visiting days his enthusiasm for his various new activities such as rowing and soccer didn't exactly ring true. And I would leave with a feeling of vague unease. But the stiff-upper-lip attitude I had inherited from my own father and the code of behaviour prevalent in public-school boys at the time precluded any discussion, and I would return to London convincing myself that all was well.

Re-reading some of his letters from this time, I see that he gave very little away. 'Everything is fine here . . . I think I may be in the Trial Eight next week, but I really find soccer more fun. I played in the Junior the other day – playing the best team. They got three goals in the first half, then in the second Dubes and Wedd and I started organising everyone and we got three goals in a row. It just shows what a little shouting will do.' In another he lists his favourite authors, 'Auberon Waugh, P. G. Wodehouse and Le Carré . . . I'm taking reading very seriously now, also my style of writing. I want to write two books, one about Eton – the different stages in a boy's life here, his different attitudes to life, sex, etc., and the way they change. I also want to write a funny-bitter book attacking the Christian idea of God and morality, but I'm not sure if I could manage the latter, yet anyhow. How is your book going?' At the time I was writing a political satire – all in dialogue and based on telephone conversations between politicians, wives, mistresses, journalists and friends, which was eventually published under the title *Tell Me, Honestly*.

Towards the end of his time at Eton he was in the Eight, and head of his house. But in spite of being part of the school establishment, he was moving further away from it. I suppose the political atmosphere in the family was left of centre, but Pete was very much a child of the sixties – anti-Vietnam war, pro the hippy culture and the legalisation of cannabis.

I can't remember ever having a row with my son. As he grew older, we'd have endless arguments about politics, religion and education, but in the end we would always agree to disagree. With the girls it was different. There would be constant flare-ups, sulks and furious scenes – particularly when they were going through their early teens and a stream of shy or surly long-haired youths used to wander through the house completely ignoring me, at best, or, at worst, treating me like an interloper.

The second turning-point in our relationship was when Pete developed a life-threatening illness of the colon. He was at Cambridge at the time, reading law. The moment when the specialist at the Westminster Hospital showed me the X-rays was the worst of my life. How could this horrible disease be happening to my son? Pete was put on cortisone until he was fit enough to be operated on, but we were warned by the surgeon that this was a very experimental operation with only a low success-rate. Peter's bravery at this time was almost the hardest thing to bear. He would crack jokes with us and the surgeon, trying, I know, to give us the courage to cope. That first operation was successful but was followed by three more during the course of a year. In between he was released from hospital to recover enough strength to be ready for the next attempt.

His hospital room began to resemble an illustration by Heath Robinson as more and more devices and tubes were connected from machines to his body. The walk from our house in Chelsea to the Westminster was covered so often that I could have done it blindfold. Pete later told me that he only had to look at the expression on my face after the latest operation to know whether it had succeeded or failed. At the end of the year the brilliant surgeon and, as he emphasised, Pete's tenacity, won through, and Pete made a complete recovery. He never completed his three years at Cambridge, but he was given an Aegrotat (the equivalent to a degree) on his previous work, which enabled him to take an MA in criminology at Keele University.

It seems to contradict the truism, but I believe that if two people have been through a traumatic experience together, it doesn't necessarily bring them closer. I think that because Pete wanted to take up the reins of his life again, and allow time for the mental and physical healing process to continue, he had to detach himself a little from his family.

In any case, geography dictated this separation. Although studying at Keele, Pete was living in a cottage on the estate of Quentin Crewe with only a mongrel called Henry for company. In a letter he wrote, 'Everything is fine with me . . . the Rayburn is very good and cheap to run. A cow-man and his wife live next door, both very sweet and she's doing all my washing for me. The local village shop has incredible country butter and tomatoes that taste like the ones in Spain and I help myself to milk straight out of the milking-machine at the farm (for free) so that life could hardly be better. Sue (Crewe) has managed to find some people half a mile away who need a seventeen-hand ex-racehorse exercised regularly. . . . We had a preliminary meeting at the University on Thursday at which nothing much happened (except I discovered that everyone on the course is male, alas!). We appear to have about nine hours' teaching a week, plus visits every Tuesday. Tomorrow we go to a local borstal (home ground for me!). . . . I've got a lot of reading to do, everything changes pretty fast in criminology. Still I'm happy in my cottage – great luxury really.'

In the meantime our own lifestyle had changed dramatically. Six years previously at the age of thirty-eight, Julian had become chairman of the nationalised Steel Corporation and was finding the job an enormous challenge and responsibility. He needed all the help I could give him, and we travelled intensively, visiting steel plants all over the world and attending top-level meetings with other steel industry chairmen. I have photographs of myself in a hard helmet standing by a blast furnace in Teeside and launching a vast tanker in Nagasaki, showing the Queen and Prince Philip round a new plant at Port Talbot, and greeting the Prime Minister, Ted Heath, at the Mansion House. We attended grand dinners at Buckingham Palace and Windsor Castle, had a chauffeur-driven car and flew everywhere in private aircraft.

The only thing that didn't change was life at the farm, and I still tried to be there for the girls' school holidays. They both, at different stages, became frenetically competitive members of the local pony club, and we would drive for miles across Norfolk trailing the horsebox behind us, hunting for the elusive rosettes of yellow, blue and red. I developed a passion for gardening and got enormous pleasure from fighting the Norfolk winds and stony soil and finding old-fashioned roses, lilac, honeysuckle and wisteria tough enough to thrive in impossible conditions.

Pete had always loved the farm and tried to join us as often as he could. When he left Keele he was halfway through the process of being accepted for training as a probation officer, but he decided to accept a grant from the Social Science Research Council to do three years' research at the Institute of Psychiatry in their Addiction Unit. He had also started seeing the beautiful Cassandra, his schoolboy flame, once again. If my life hadn't been so full I might have felt a twinge of jealousy at this breaking of the umbilical bond – but, in any case, I had always believed they were completely right for each other.

Just as life seemed to be on an even course at last, Pete's father died of a heart attack in Majorca. He was forty-eight. The traumatic shock and grief for us all are not part of this story. But obviously it changed all our lives fundamentally and, once again, as before when Pete was a small eight-year-old, I turned to him for support. He, in turn, was fighting his own battles. In an extract from a long letter he sent me a few months later he wrote: 'I will do everything I can to make your life easier in the next few months and years; I hope that you will help me assert myself, make decisions and play the role that I must in the future. The way life goes small things are bound to upset people, and we are bound to upset each other, me more than you, I'm sure. I hope and pray that this won't ever come between us, things never have in the past and I feel I need your support more now than I ever have.'

After the burial service in the grim family mausoleum in north London, there was a memorial service at Westminster Abbey. Very soon afterwards Pete was asked when he would be taking his seat in the House of Lords. This he was very reluctant to do, believing that a future Labour Party should abolish the hereditary system. But he was persuaded by me and a close family friend, a peer, Eddy Shackleton, that the best way to fight for his beliefs was from within the establishment.

Pete made no concessions in his lifestyle and would ride to the Lords on his bike, leaving it in the peers' car-park and putting on a tie as he passed the top-hatted attendants. He soon became completely at ease with the formalities of the Upper House and began to make a reputation as a formidable speaker and committed socialist. When I sat in the Peeresses' Gallery listening to him and watching the tall, authoritative figure of a man, I could hardly believe this was the same delicate child I had worried over in the control tower in Norfolk.

He left the Institute of Psychiatry only when the Prime Minister, Harold Wilson, asked him to join his government. Later, Wilson told me he had been a little reluctant as, until then, he himself had the record of being the youngest minister. Meanwhile, I was trying to build a new life for myself while still living in the same house in Chelsea with my younger daughter, Pandora. Kerena, a talented musician, had opted out of university and instead had become a bit of a groupie, following her favourite pop idols to distant spots. She recovered from this phase when she met her future husband, Richard Moorehead. She lived with him in Norfolk, where she took a degree in Development Studies at the University of East Anglia.

Pandora was a day girl at St Paul's. She was going through an uncommunicative phase, retreating into her own shell of grief. Returning from school she would go to her bedroom and play her stereo at a deafening volume. The room began to look like a corner of a refugee camp. Cigarettes were squashed into half-empty coffee mugs and the wastepaper basket brimmed over with laddered tights. One day I could stand it no longer and, stepping through the piles of dirty clothes on the floor, I tried to create a little cleanliness and order. While sorting out the clothes to be washed, I picked up a plastic bag with a small amount of dark-brown grains at the bottom. Thinking the worst and sick with worry, I telephoned Pete. He suggested we meet for lunch that day at the Lords. When I told him that I was terrified his sister was on drugs, he asked to see the offending article. 'Surely not here,' I said, looking nervously at a purple-robed bishop sitting at the next table. 'Why not? No one would expect us to be examining an illegal substance under the eyes of the bishop.' I produced the evidence from my bag and Pete bent down, pretending to do up his shoelace, and smelt it. His eyes were twinkling as he looked up. 'Coffee,' he said. 'She probably doesn't like the Nescafé at school. Serves you right for being so suspicious.'

I was now on the board of the Royal Court Theatre and later of the National Theatre, and trying to do some writing – journalism, interviews and travel pieces. Pete and I were going our separate ways and sometimes we wouldn't be in contact for months. He was sent to Ireland as a junior minister, and I once visited him in Stormont Castle expecting it to be very grand, but I found it divided up into small, dreary offices and living-quarters.

When Pete came home, he and Cassandra decided to set up a home together in north London, and at the fall of the Labour government in 1979 he was free to follow what had become his true passion – conservation. He was first president of the Ramblers Association and then executive director of

Greenpeace. At last he was working at a job he loved, with people he respected and in a world-wide organisation of power and influence for the preservation of our planet. As it was one of the more controversial of the pressure groups, with its actions against nuclear arms and its policies on global warming, Pete used all his political skills to maintain its political independence.

I suppose the only really serious disagreement we ever had was on a walk round Battersea Park, when he told me Cassandra was pregnant. Even if it was a son, they didn't intend to marry. He didn't believe in making vows in a church or registry office that he could equally well make in private. He didn't believe in God, disliked organised religion, thought many aspects of marriage demeaned women, and didn't believe in the hereditary principle. Having been brought up in the Church of England, I believed that my religion was part of my national heritage; it gave me a deep inner strength in spite of the fact that I was not a regular churchgoer. But when we walked round the park, this was not what we discussed in depth. I felt that, in spite of his own convictions, he should at least give freedom of choice to a son who might one day disagree with him and might wish to carry on the Melchett name and all it stood for. Peter argued that if he wasn't strong enough to convince his own son of his beliefs, he wouldn't be much good as a father. As we circled the park, round and round went the arguments, which I knew Pete would win in the end, as he always did. But I was convinced it was my duty to put the case as strongly as I could for his dead father and, indeed, for his unborn son. I don't know how long we walked and talked, but it was growing dark and the gates were closing.

And that was the last time the issue of the hereditary title was mentioned between us.

Cassandra had a daughter and, two years later, a son. Pete is a model of the 'new age father' and adored by his children, who seem to have adopted his beliefs and philosophy. One aspect of their upbringing somewhat amused me. Pete stood more for environmental influences than for heredity in the forming of children's outlook and character. He believed that if you brought up male and female children in exactly the same way, they would become less aggressively male or female. So boys should not be given guns and cars to play with, nor girls dolls. I only know that whatever was actually put into practice, Jay is a very masculine boy and Jessy as feminine as possible. But I'm sure if I brought it up, Pete would have a good defence.

Eleven years had elapsed after my first husband's death when I met the man I was to marry – the historian and writer Andrew Sinclair, who had two sons of his own. My children were delighted to see me really happy once again and they all get on extremely well with their stepfather – as I, after a few false starts, do with my stepsons. Rather to his surprise, Andrew has become the patriarchal figure of an extended family – a role he secretly enjoys, and he is far better with the grandchildren than I am. He makes music boxes when not writing books, and he has a wonderful collection of old toys which he and the children play with for hours.

Pete is now somewhat of a public figure with a demanding and busy life. When we meet, which is far too infrequently, we still agree to disagree on a variety of subjects. I'm sure I'm not as politically correct as he would wish. I'm not a vegetarian as he is, nor do I use recycled paper, and when I finish a bottle of wine I don't put it in a bottle bank. He once made me sign away all my bodily organs on my death to the local hospital. I thought it a bit macabre at the time, but I'm sure he was right.

Because we both now lead very full and active lives we don't see each other as much as we would wish. But I believe that the mother–son relationship is extraordinarily strong – as D. H. Lawrence (one of Pete's favourite authors as a boy) described so vividly. It goes through many metamorphoses, but if you are lucky, as I have been, it never changes in essence. I even saw my present husband return to being an obedient little boy at his tiny but dominating mother's slightest demand. In our case Pete has his hands full with his job, his family, his friends and running the farm. I'm sure he is relieved that, knowing I'm in excellent hands, he can put me to the back of his mind and needn't have any worries about me. Neither of us is nostalgic, nor do we live in the past. Who knows what even the next twenty-four hours will bring? But I do know that I can always turn to him in times of stress for help and support, and that he would never let me down.

*B*lind *B*itter *H*appiness

A DAM   M ARS-J ONES

Adam Mars-Jones' books are Lantern Lecture,
Monopolies of Loss *and* The Waters of Thirst.
Since 1986 he has reviewed films for the
Independent, *and contributes regularly to* The Times
Literary Supplement *and* The London Review
of Books.

My mother was born on 20 August 1923, and christened
Sheila Mary Felicity Cobon. At some stage she was told the
supposed meaning of these names, or looked them up in a
book. Her forenames meant by derivation 'Blind Bitter
Happiness'. As an adult Sheila found this augury ruefully
amusing or faintly annoying, in its mixture of the appropriate
and the hopelessly wrong.

Sheila was both a wanted and an unwanted child. Charles
and Gladys Cobon already had a daughter, three-year-old
Margaret ('Peggy'). What they wanted was not Sheila, the
eventual alto, but a boy, who would in time sing treble in the
same choir as his father. There was a name prepared for the

invited guest: Derek. Sheila was a failed Derek, a fact which was not entirely kept from her.

She was keenly aware of the difference in status, as far as her father was concerned, between herself and her sister. The family lived in Wembley, while Charles worked for a firm of marine engineers in Rotherhithe. As a matter of routine, Peggy would meet Charles's train after work on a Saturday. When Sheila was old enough to deputise for her sister in this coveted duty, Charles's first question would always be: 'Is Peggy ill?' This was before parenting skills. He didn't have the sense to wrap it up. To say: 'Lovely to see you, Sheila. Kind of you to come and meet your old man. How's your mother? Good, good. And Peggy?'

As children, Peggy and Sheila competed over such important matters as who could eat slowest. Peggy was particularly skilled at hiding, say, a straggling line of peas in the shadow of a folded knife and fork, so as to thwart Sheila's triumph and eat the stragglers with a relish out of all proportion to their deliciousness.

As a girl, Sheila's candidates for the title of Naughtiest Words in the World were 'bosom' and 'spasm'. She would say them in her head continuously, until the laughter burst out of her. Bosom spasm bosom spasm. A litany of taboos. A wicked prayer.

Sheila was ten when Gladys died, after a stroke, and it was Sheila who found her, stricken, incapable, labouring for breath.

Ever after, Sheila was hysterically distressed by physical impairment, by paralysis and mutilation, even the malformation of a London pigeon's feet. A pigeon with fused feet was still a wounded bird to her, a fly-specked mirror held up to her of bedraggled suffering, loss of self. Her reaction was complex, being made up of both identification and disgust, the desire for things to be whole and for them to be dead. If anyone asked about this phobic affinity, she would refer to the conspicuous presence in her childhood of veterans injured in the war, but not everyone of her generation was so deeply affected.

In the months after her mother died, a new routine established itself. Sheila would come home from school first and let herself in, but was not trusted to make a fire on her own or for her own benefit. She had to wait for Peggy's return before she could think of getting warm.

When Charles himself returned, he would cook supper, which would be chops or else steak, and boiled potatoes. Sheila was in a phase of revulsion against meat, and ate only the potatoes. At weekends the girls' Aunt Mimi, who lived in Rotherhithe, would cook Sunday lunch and prepare sandwiches for them to eat at school the next day, using the meat left over. On the way home Sheila would be revulsed all over again, seeing the wrapped sandwiches in the glove compartment of the car. She was prone to carsickness anyway, but the closeness of the meat made things worse. At school she would throw the meat away, convinced it smelt of petrol, and eat only the bread.

Those around her did not for some time connect the fact of her developing boils with her near-exclusive diet of bread and potatoes.

Charles was not a worldly man. His father had been an organist and had published a *Te Deum*: Charles himself not only sang in the choir but was a lay preacher. If he had a passion beside God and marine engineering, it was trains. He didn't share his bereavement with his daughters, but then bereavement is not for sharing. If it can be shared, it is something other than bereavement. Still, Charles can't be accused of anticipating his children's needs with overmuch imagination. He did know, though, that girls need a mother. He found one for them.

Lilian, his second wife, was a schoolteacher in her forties. Her motives for the union are more obscure than her new husband's. Perhaps there was sly triumph in the casting off of a maiden name, at a time of life when the label 'Old Maid' was firmly attached to her. Perhaps, too, as a teacher who had met the Cobon girls in their mother's lifetime, she responded to Charles's appeal on their behalf, and to the challenge of shaping a child's character more directly than she could in the classroom.

It was 'a child' she had ambitions to shape, rather than children, and her first choice was Peggy. She would have had more of a chance if she had played her cards better. It was a mistake to insist that the girls both wear ankle socks and frilled red velvet dresses at the wedding. Peggy at fourteen thought herself too grown-up to be dressed as a child, almost a doll, and never forgave the ankle socks.

It was also a mistake to expect to be called Mummie, or at least to make an issue of it. Peggy would never call Lilian Mummie. Sheila would.

Now at least there was someone who noticed whether she ate properly or not. Boils stood no chance against Lilian. Lilian was also determined that Sheila should have a proper education, and in due course be financially independent.

This was in part a recognition that Sheila was bright, but also reflected a colder agenda. It was Lilian's feeling that women should always be financially independent, because women should have as little as possible to do with men in any way.

By the time she was fourteen, Sheila had been told by Lilian that she had never let Charles come near her in 'that way'. No carnal congress for Lilian, thank you very much. No bosom spasm.

What did Lilian think she was doing by passing on so grotesquely inappropriate a confidence? There are a number of possibilities. To establish as a general principle that Men Are Beasts. Or to offer reassurance that she was playing by the rules of the marriage: the girls' new mother, not Charles's new wife. Perhaps, too, it was a way of striking a bargain. Showing that she had no secrets from Sheila – a rare sort of trust. And trust must be returned.

By being mother of a sort to at least one of his children, without being functionally Charles's wife, Lilian effectively split the family in two. At one point she had a maid who performed some duties also for Sheila, but had instructions not to attend on Charles or Peggy. From there it was only a small step to separate the two half-households.

In her early teens Sheila was not expected to choose what clothes to wear – she put on what was laid out for her, school-day or holiday. So there could be no question of her being allowed to choose which person to live with. Lilian always said that when she was sixteen Sheila would be able to exercise a choice, but it was clear that Lilian had fixed expectations of the choice.

Looking back as an adult (and a legally trained adult to boot), Sheila realised that Lilian was careful all this time to avoid making herself vulnerable to a charge of deserting Charles. What she wanted was to negotiate her demands from within the married state, not risk a departure from it. So Sheila would spend the time after school at Lilian's mother's house, 92 Upward Road, and then be brought back to sleep in the family home, the house with the grandly pretty name of Foxes Dale.

The prospect of being allowed to choose somehow suggested to Sheila that she was considered relatively unimportant. Charles hardly seemed anxious to claim her. Sheila didn't even particularly look like a Cobon, unlike Peggy, with her bony face and prominent eyes.

Sheila had masses of dark curly hair, cause for pride, and a nose she felt was beaky, cause for shame. There were other things about which she felt self-conscious. Her feet were so narrow that she would leave school-issue shoes behind, even tightly laced, if she ran upstairs. The man who operated the X-ray pedoscope in the shoe shop said gravely that she would be in a wheelchair by fifty. Did he think that she had been born with wide, fat feet, and that the narrowing was progressive?

There wasn't actually a moment for Sheila of decision between guardians. Before she was ever sixteen, rights over her had imperceptibly been transferred to Lilian. She had been kidnapped piecemeal.

Sheila was too young to wonder whether the bisection of the family was a legally sanctioned or an informal arrangement. In later life she assumed it was informal, and therefore that Lilian took her because Charles didn't want to. It was not in Lilian's interest to tell her that Charles contributed to her maintenance, and that both parties had put their signatures to an Agreement as signing custody.

Lilian's care, which had from the start contained an element of over-identification, of vicarious living, shaded bit by bit into abuse. Sheila never used that word about her experience of subjection, even when it became ubiquitous in the culture, so that people could be routinely described as abusing alcohol, or a racquet during a tennis match. It was 'only' emotional abuse, moreover: but abuse it was. Lilian pumped the breathable air out of the house, and replaced it with oxides of rancour, her grudge against the world.

Lilian would give her stepdaughter the silent treatment for three uninterrupted days, until Sheila begged to be told what her crime had been. It would turn out to be misbehaviour on the level of failing, at a school concert, to let the applause die down fully before coming on stage to announce the next item. Just *bouncing* on to the stage, full of herself in a common way.

By this method Sheila's mild extroversion was obliterated. Yet she never thought of Lilian's behaviour as normal. She had memories enough of the time before her mother's death to know that it was Lilian's coldly boiling rage which was disordered. She developed a hatred of confrontations and of 'atmospheres' which has lasted all her life.

Lilian had no real prospect of imposing a hatred of men on this adolescent girl. The part of Sheila's sensibility which had been so tickled by 'bosom spasm bosom spasm' would later take joy in a school joke that Lilian would certainly have found smutty:

Girl's Father: I should inform you, young man, that the
                lights go out in this house at nine-thirty
                sharp.

Young Man: I say, Sir, that's awfully sporting!

If this was smut, it was more wholesome than what Lilian
dished up daily.

Though Sheila was not temperamentally able to assert herself against Lilian, she wasn't altogether biddable either. On
one occasion she ran away, and fulfilled an ambition fuelled by
her teenage reading by sleeping in a haystack. She loved to
read. Once she'd been so wrapped up, perched halfway up a
tree reading *Lorna Doone*, that she missed lunch, and didn't
even mind.

From Lilian's reign onwards, although Sheila was widely
regarded as bright, anyone who wanted to make her feel
stupid could do so, and there were those who produced
the same effect without intending to or noticing, purely in
passing.

One day, staying with a schoolfriend, she picked up a book
which her hostess's older brother was studying as part of his
university course. She had been given his bedroom to sleep in,
and law books were everywhere. This particular volume was
called *Winfield on Tort*. She opened the book at random, and
her eyes fell on a bracketed phrase: '(Married Women and
Tortfeasors)'. There was something irresistibly comic about
this combination – a tortfeasor sounded as if it should mean a
small spherical sweet, honeycomb with a coating of chocolate.
*I'll have a box of tortfeasors, please – they're the torts with the less fat-
tening centres.* It seemed plain to her that somewhere lurking in

the legal system was a great dry sense of humour. She read on, and found herself if not exactly rocking with laughter, then certainly intrigued by the system that the book spelt out.

Sheila was a good student, and Lilian could hardly object, in view of her stated ambitions for her stepdaughter, to the plan of reading law in due time at London University, re-located in wartime to Cambridge. Sheila and her lodgings-mate smoked five cigarettes a week each, on princi-ple. They were sending smoke signals. This was their way of signalling that they were approachable, not nuns or prudes but Modern Women.

In the evenings Sheila helped at a canteen set up for forces personnel doing courses: the bolder men called her 'the Girl with the Gypsy Eyes'.

The war brought both enlargements of horizon and set-backs to Sheila. She had especially been looking forward to the appearance of American troops in the global conflict, but in the event she was disappointed. Their buttocks were large and slack; they looked nothing like the men in the movies. Could that be why they were called 'doughboys'?

In June 1943, when Sheila was nineteen, Lilian made some sort of appeal to Charles, desiring him to reinforce her authority with his. It was odd that she should make such an approach, when she had hitherto been so steadfast in separat-ing father and daughter.

Charles had come to regret the Agreement that gave Lilian her power, and seems to have suggested that Sheila should return to his care, if she was proving troublesome. Lilian's response to Charles's solicitors was sharp. She would of course continue to respect the Agreement, and to offer Sheila parental affection as and when she proved worthy of it. It was not possible, however, to offer care to a headstrong young woman who was abetted in her opposition by outsiders. She was disgusted by the motive of Mr Cobon's interference. If she had known he would seek to exploit the situation she would never have thought of involving him.

Charles asked his solicitors if there was any prospect of having the Agreement set aside. They told him this would only be possible by mutual consent, while in this matter the parties hardly seemed to be *ad idem*. By professional reflex they translated the idea of being in agreement into the dignified extinction of Latin. They did, however, object to Mrs Cobon's withholding information about Sheila's whereabouts, information to which he was certainly entitled.

After that, Charles adopted a more conciliatory, even wheedling approach. He started his letters 'Dear Lily', and wrote a rough draft so that he could add a little more soap to the final version. He was grateful that she was doing so much for Sheila. He would send any gifts or pocket money to Lily rather than Sheila, for her to pass on as she saw fit. He would be grateful for an opportunity of seeing Sheila, in London if that was more agreeable to Lily. Perhaps he could take her to a show. He would of course meet all expenses.

Between the ages of fifteen and twenty-five, Sheila saw her father twice, and her sister not at all. The estrangement extended even to birthday and Christmas cards. The second lunch, when she was nineteen or so, was perhaps the rendezvous requested in the letter to Lilian. Charles surprised his daughter by treating her as a grown-up. This recognition was conveyed by the offer of a glass of light ale.

Charles kept the correspondence that had been conducted through his solicitors, and also the drafts of his letters of entreaty. After his death in 1980, aged ninety-four, they passed to Peggy, who rather oddly, since there was no bad blood between the sisters, didn't show them to the person they chiefly concerned.

There was no testamentary reference to the letters, so no direct duty was owed. Peggy had lived with and looked after her father all her life, though even in old age he had an independent streak. He would usually cook the dinner (steak or chops), took short holidays on his own even in his nineties, and wasn't above directing the occasional perfunctory kick at the current embodiment of Peggy's love for emotionally inadequate dogs. Quite properly she inherited the bulk of his modest estate.

So why hang on to those letters? It was as if she was back with the ingrained competitiveness of the nursery, hiding peas on her dinner plate from Sheila one last time. Only after Peggy's own death, in November 1995, did the letters, with their fragmentary story of an attempt to reverse an abandonment, find their way to Sheila. Even then she was shy of them, not in a hurry to learn what they implied.

After Part One of her degree, Sheila joined the Wrens, and was duly posted to a Wrennery in London. The premises were very grand, a town house in Cheyne Walk, and she slept in the ballroom, but she shared it with thirty-one other Wrens. Sixteen of them would want the windows open at night, and sixteen wanted them shut, so half of them were always simmeringly resentful. They were a mixed group: one girl never changed her clothes, until eventually they had to be taken from her by a little deputation of hygienic Wrens. A kangaroo court, come to lynch a dirty shirt.

There was drudgery, admittedly, in the effort to keep smart. You had to wash your white shirt every night, and iron it in the morning, either getting up at crack of dawn or queuing for the iron. Then after breakfast Sheila would walk across the bridge to Battersea and learn how to assemble radios. Luckily her hair was short: girls with long hair were always having it brush against the soldering iron. The smell of burnt hair became familiar, almost consoling. In the evenings she would do her Bates exercises, for perfect sight without glasses, before washing her shirt again. If the exercises had worked for Aldous Huxley, who had been as good as blind, why not for her?

Lilian's plan to make Sheila a career woman, independent of men, had the inherent drawback that the world of work was full of them. After the war and the completion of her degree, she was called to Gray's Inn as a barrister. By the time she met Bill Mars-Jones in 1946, it was no novelty to be romanced by a stranger.

He projected on to her a strongly romantic account of their future together. But he also — and this *was* a novelty — seemed bothered by his lost virginity, and introduced the subject with a jarring urgency into their early conversations. Why in the world does he think I care one way or the other? she thought. She also found it odd, if virginity was so important to him, that he seemed to entertain no doubts whatever about her own. This was almost unflattering enough to pique an interest. Did he think she'd had no offers?

Still, he had merits. One of them was that although he had served, and even earned a rather smart little gong, he didn't go

on and on about the war, the way so many men did. Maybe
that was an advantage of the navy, that either everyone went
down together or they were all more or less OK. You could
see action without seeing casualties directly, without being
scarred or turned into some dreary hero. Bill had had his
share of dangerous duty, on Russian convoys, but his closest
brush with death proper came when he was posted to HMS
Hood, sunk before he could take up the post.

It was almost a shock when Bill turned out to be Welsh.
He'd lost the accent in pretty short order. His voice was musical, but he sounded more like someone on the Home Service
than a country boy who was going to say 'look you' at the
drop of a hat. Perhaps she had met the only Welshman in
London at that time who didn't dream of being mistaken for
Dylan Thomas.

Bill was still thrilled to be living in London, which made
Sheila feel almost old, but in a nice way. Bill was still, deep
down, the teenager who had hidden his face in fear at a
screening of *King Kong* on his first visit to London, grateful to
have his father sitting next to him – not because the old man
made him feel strong by example, rather the opposite. His
Dad gave little suppressed yelps during the great ape's appear-
ances, and prayed under his breath in Welsh.

Bill was smartly dressed, even a bit of a dandy, what with
his tie always in a tubby Windsor knot, but it was pretty clear
he wasn't a wolf. From the way he told her about his past phi-
landering, it was clear that a philanderer was what he was not.

It was only much later, on her first visit to Bill's family in
North Wales, that she understood some of the fuss about his
fallen sexual state. He came from a different world. She had

been briefed to do without make-up and cigarettes, at least until Bill's widowed father got to know her. It was bad enough her being English rather than Welsh, without being *painted* and English, and the smoke signals that spelt out Modern Womanhood in Cambridge would convey the same all-too-inflammatory message here.

In Bill's world, the woman you married would be as pure as your mother had been – and he had mourned his mother intensely. Most men of twenty-one (his age at the time of bereavement) have passed the stage of thinking that their mother is a truly perfect being, but Bill had not. He had been unable to sleep at home when his loss was raw, and families in the village had taken him in for a few nights at a time, on a rota basis, until he could bear to return. The dead woman had been popular, but still there was an element of bafflement at Bill's behaviour, at his taking on so.

Bill would have it that his intended recapitulated his mother's virtues. She was entitled to expect a virgin, and he broke the bad news to her as soon as possible, before he lost his nerve. Never mind that his seduction technique with local girls had been not only rather successful but rather calculating: day-trips by rail to Manchester with their parents' permission, without chaperonage since no night away was involved. A brisk poke in an unshared compartment, with no fear – on a train without a corridor – of being seen. Getting into trouble precluded by a protective from Denbigh's leading dealer in rubber goods, a tradesman known to all as Lord Dunlop.

Impossible to go into these coarse details with someone of Sheila's refinement (whose railway-related adventures, by contrast, had tended to involve artificially missing the last train).

Nor did Sheila learn until much later that there had been a particular urgency in Bill's desire to get married. Looking at his hairbrush one day, he found it matted with shed fibres, and convinced himself he was going rapidly bald. He was already thirty, after all, and his younger brother David had gone bald in his twenties (admittedly David had made matters worse by forever wearing a cap).

Their mother was all but bald, or she had been until the day of her Transformation. One day Father had said, 'Your mother has had a Transformation,' and when Mam had come downstairs, radiantly smiling, the top of her head had a quite different aspect. No one in Llansannan used the word 'wig'. Perhaps no one even thought it. It was always 'Your Mam's Transformation is so smart', 'Doesn't your Mam look magnificent in her Transformation?' The sudden change in Mrs Jones's appearance was received in that Chapel community like a biblical miracle. It was not to be questioned. Lazarus was dead and just now came stumbling from the tomb. Mrs Jones was all but bald and now has a fine head of hair.

Still, Bill thought he'd better get married, just to be on the safe side, rather than rely on a miracle. Better get a girl down the aisle while there was still some thatch remaining. So Bill looked through his address book, in search of women who were potentially marriageable, women in other words who had turned him down sexually. It wasn't much of a list.

If in fact Bill's hair had given him cause for concern, it must have been that he was going through some sort of seasonal moult. He continued to produce scalp fur in large quantities. Or perhaps it was that being married acted as a hair restorative. In later life Sheila, watching him brush it with daily devotedness, would experience a rueful twinge. Hospitalised for an intestinal abscess in 1995, Bill would sweetly ignore requests to do physiotherapy, but would brush his hair for hours.

As a young man, Bill was known for his charm. He played the guitar, and would improvise comical calypsos at parties. At university (Aberystwyth and then Cambridge) he had done as much acting as studying: his advocacy was a professionally promising mixture of careful preparation and theatrical flair.

He seemed so very sure that he had found the right woman, and who was Sheila to say he was wrong? Her extroversion was a shadow of its former self after the Lilian years, and she never found it easy to make the first move. With Bill, she might never have to. Very early on in their relationship, Bill started relying on her to prompt his patchy memory, to remember the names and histories of his friends – including those she hadn't met! She experienced a twinge of irritation flooded out by the joy of being needed, a combination of emotions she recognised as promisingly marital.

If Bill's father had taken to Sheila, despite Bill's fears, no such rapport could be expected between Bill and Lilian. Learning that Bill's father was a lifelong teetotaller, she wrote to him warning him that his son had a serious drinking problem. She did however agree, when this revelation seemed to have no effect on the proposed union, to take on the traditional duties of the bride's mother.

Her motive, though, was sabotage. She consented to Sheila's father attending, but Peggy received no invitation. The list of Bill's guests was firmly restricted.

Sheila was given away not by her father but by her Uncle

Harry. Uncle Harry, a civil servant, could not quite grasp the concept of the bride's tactical lateness on her defining day. All Sheila's procrastination could not succeed in making her more than a little late, and she had the symbolic humiliation of arriving earlier than her groom. Bill and the best man, his brother David, had stopped off for a quick one – a sharpener, a dose of 'lotion' – on the way to the church.

Sheila trembled so badly during the ceremony that she thought everyone must notice. She was sure her wedding dress was shaking right down to its train. When the ceremony was safely over and she arrived at the reception, a waiter offered her a mixed drink. Accepting, she asked what it was. The drink was so potent and so timely that it took away all her tension, but as it did so it took away also the name of this utterly necessary, utterly restoring drink. She was never able to remember what it was.

At the reception Bill's father, a teetotaller but not a fool, fixed Lilian in the eye while he drank a glass of champagne, without visible distress. But perhaps the sparkling wine in his glass was changed, as he drank it, into untroubling water: a reversed miracle-at-Cana, reworked with abstainers in mind.

Sheila hated the photographs of herself at the wedding and destroyed them. She did, however, permit the pictures of the couple in going-away clothes after the reception to continue to exist.

The newlyweds honeymooned in Ireland. For the first time Sheila ate potatoes that had been boiled in their jackets, a simple pleasure. They went to the Abbey Theatre, a sophisticated one.

Bill had been in charge of the arrangements and had got

the dates wrong, so the marriage got under way not in the intended suite but in the only room their Dublin hotel had free for the first night: an attic room whose bed had comically squeaky springs. A prop from a bad farce, not the sort of theatrical fare for people who bought tickets for the Abbey.

On the way back from Ireland the two of them spent two nights with Bill's father and (fair's fair) two nights with Lilian. Lilian, however, had moved from attempted sabotage to a sort of flailing revenge, and claimed back from Sheila every present she had given her over the previous decade and a half. There was a particularly undignified squabble over a pair of ice-skates that were too small for Sheila anyway, but had not become quite worthless to either party.

Lilian unleashed revenge on a new front by sending the invoices for the wedding and reception expenses to the groom. Bill got the bill. This was a particular imposition since the newlyweds' assets at the time of their marriage amounted to (this is the statutory phrasing) two briefcases, two umbrellas and a thousand-pound overdraft. As an index of the ominousness of that figure: the rent at Clare Court, their first home, was three pounds a week.

Bill had stayed with a friend for a few days before his wedding, learning how to cook. What he learnt how to cook was bacon and eggs, which he prepared for Sheila on Sunday mornings in the first year of their marriage.

Despite everything, Sheila didn't cleanly break with Lilian. Perhaps she felt free enough of that influence to be magnanimous. Perhaps she was beginning, even, to feel pity. Lilian came to call while Bill was away on circuit, and warned her fiercely of the danger she was in from poisoning. She must avoid eating anything that Bill had prepared or even touched.

Luckily, one weekend Bill was so tired that Sheila cooked breakfast for him, and he never offered again. The danger of poisoning at his hands, never great, dwindled to nothing.

In the summer of 1949 Bill and Sheila took a holiday in Spain. Sheila was the linguist of the couple, but had only basic Italian to make stretch so as to fit this rather different country. She had brought with her a new bathing-suit, which was smart by British standards, but, as she saw on her first visit to the swimming beach, was potentially a scandal in Franco's Spain. It wasn't remotely a bikini – bikinis didn't exist – but it *was* a two-piece, and Fascist beachwear had not yet taken that path. The señoras chose to veil their mid-sections, while Sheila felt much more self-conscious about her (as she thought) knobbly knees than about her firm young midriff.

She felt less conspicuous when she was actually in the water, and undertook to give Bill a long-overdue lesson in floating. Bill swam short distances with vigour, especially if women were watching, but had not yet learnt to suppress the panic reflex that prevents relaxed floating, particularly when he was out of his depth. She tried to persuade him to put his trust in the basic unsinkability of the body.

Rather than run into town and buy a less challenging costume, Sheila and Bill decided the next day to find another beach. Sheila thought she had seen a party of nuns take to the water in the next bay. They would swim there. With them went a hotel acquaintance who had been a champion swimmer not so long ago.

The sea was rough, and thanks to the unfamiliar pleasure of being knocked off balance by big brusque waves they didn't immediately realise that they were being swept out and were out of their depth almost at once. As it turned out, the beach was notorious locally for its appetite, and the nuns glimpsed the day before were optical illusions, or else only paddling.

The hotel acquaintance resolved to swim back to shore and raise the alarm. Bill and Sheila needed only to stay afloat. They were soon separated in the water, however, and Sheila, knowing that floating was a very shallowly rooted skill in Bill's repertoire, gave him up for dead. Mentally she was widowed as she trod water in the heavy swell, waiting for death or rescue. She had time to absorb the full meaning of the phrase 'lost at sea'.

The third member of the party managed with difficulty to reach the shore. He tried to explain the situation to the few people on the beach. One of them was a young man called Xavier Cremades, who as soon as he understood seized a child's inflatable boat – a tiny thing, only a toy – and charged into the water. He let himself be swept out in his turn, reasoning that this would bring him to the approximate position of the floundering English.

If Sheila had been visualising rescue, it was not in the form of what looked like a teenager holding on to an inflated toy boat rather smaller than an airbed. She had left her glasses with her towel and her book on the beach, but she had no difficulty seeing him approach. Her first thought was, What a clot! What a clot to be out in this sea with that cockleshell.

Then he swam up to her, and she realised that if this was a clot she should be thankful for it. He was nodding and smiling, having no English and prevented from gesticulating by the need to hold on to the infant lifeboat. Sheila gestured wildly in all directions at the heaving sea, shouting hoarsely, *'Il marito!'* This was Italian, and she conscientiously repeated her distress signal in what she hoped was the corresponding Spanish idiom: *'El marido!'* Xavier Cremades had understood the first time, and the two of them started to search together.

Of course he wasn't Xavier Cremades to her then, simply a figure as unlikely and as inherently sunlit as a boy on a dolphin.

Each of them now held on to the little boat, and when a swell lifted them briefly up they tried to stare at different sectors of what was revealed to them. Sheila's eyes were less sharp than Xavier's, but she had the advantage of having a clearer mental image of what they were looking for: his dear hair matted with seaweed, the view of his pale back under the water that would mean he had forgotten yesterday's lesson in floating.

Bill was actually only a little distance away, unconscious and blue in the face but undeniably floating. Without being able to communicate verbally, Sheila and Xavier nevertheless managed a very tricky piece of manoeuvring. At this point the boat expands from its previously stated dimensions, and becomes big enough for a woman and a boy to heave an unconscious man on to it. So be it. Or compromise by saying that what they were doing, despite the emphasis on teamwork and heaving, was closer to slipping the boat underneath Bill, with the same happy result of flotation.

Sheila didn't dare to hope that Bill would be all right, even now. She had no way of knowing how much water he had swallowed, but at least he was breathing. On he breathed. She wanted him to cough, to clear his lungs of what they had taken in, and she managed with Xavier's help to turn him face down so he could safely vomit. For any more ambitious rendering of first aid, the little boat would have had to go through another, more drastic expansion, to the size of the vessel that eventually rescued them, a ship of the Spanish navy.

Bill, Sheila and Xavier Cremades were briefly local celebrities. Some of the speculation was romantic – the English couple mistakenly thought to be honeymooners – and some of it mildly prurient. What sort of bathing-suit would make even a foreigner have second thoughts?

The parents of Xavier Cremades gave a little reception in honour of the rescued visitors, once Bill had recovered. It might have been expected that any entertaining should be the other way about, which only made the gesture more charming. Pride, too, has a right to a party.

The event was announced as a tea and took place at the appropriate hour, but Bill in particular was pleasantly surprised by the Spanish interpretation of the meal, in which sherry of many different styles was served in tiny glasses. Tea the liquid featured only by special request. In that period of intense currency restrictions, this was a bash that few British tourists who hadn't been lucky enough to near-drown could hope for.

Bill was the one who had been despaired of, but Sheila took much longer to recover. Bill, after all, had known nothing of being despaired of, while Sheila's despair as she trod water out of sight of land, her sense of being rescued from Lilian and then abandoned all over again, had been an overwhelming mental event.

Back in London, with Bill away on circuit, Sheila started to show the early symptoms of some sort of breakdown. She was prey to obsessional thoughts. Sitting on a bus, she would be aware of people looking at her oddly, and only then realise that she had been silently weeping for some considerable time.

Medical advice was sought on her behalf: her state of anxiety was diagnosed, perhaps unsurprisingly, as an anxiety state. Being given a description and a name for what she was experiencing did her some small good in itself. The suggestion was made that she was reliving, in an oblique way, the marine despair she had experienced before Xavier Cremades paddled into view, of which she had no direct memory. Time would bring a cure, time that steals all wounds.

It became increasingly difficult for Sheila to let Bill out of her sight, and for a while she stayed with him on circuit. Bill's professional life, though, with its institutionalised male camaraderie of Circuit Mess and Circuit Dinners, its heavy smoking and drinking and sessions of frantic preparation through the night, was essentially a bachelor zone in a married life, and Sheila couldn't indefinitely share it.

Her symptoms gradually abated, but the simmering of her brain as it cooled percolated through to her skin, and a few months after Spain she started to suffer from psoriasis. Stress is recognised to play a part in this condition. From then on, her quest for clear skin took over from any direct quest for emotional peace. Over the years, she tried a number of remedies, from acupuncture and PUVA-plus-sunlamp to (in the 1970s) methotrexate, which proved the most effective treatment for a condition which was never as obvious to others as it was to her. But why is that always offered as a consolation? To say the same thing with a different emphasis: it was a condition that impinged on her sense of herself as much as it affected her dermis.

Sheila had never wanted children, partly because every baby whose pram she had ever leant over lost no time in bursting into tears. Bill, however, had always made clear that he had a paternal destiny, and wanted four sons. Eventually, after a few years of marriage, Sheila leant over a friend's pram and was greeted with a gurgle rather than a howl. It seemed to her that a jinx had been lifted. Perhaps children of her own would gurgle too.

Though she had never wanted children, it hadn't occurred to Sheila that they wouldn't come when they were called. They tried. They monitored cycles and ringed dates on the calendar. On one occasion Bill was away on circuit, appearing in an important case, for almost the entirety of Sheila's time of ripeness. He would be cutting it fine. Never short of bravado or a lawyer's access to official favours, he arranged for a police car to meet his train at Paddington. The fretful sperm travelled under police escort as it went to meet the shivering egg.

Nothing worked. Every time they had 'tried' early in the day, Bill and Sheila would catch a show, hoping to cheer themselves up. But that year in the theatre the controlling metaphor of every play seemed to be infertility. Every time they sat down in the stalls, the curtain rose to show them a childless couple symbolising the emptiness at the heart of modern life.

Bill took tests, and so did Sheila. She knew she had only one Fallopian tube, since the other had become gangrenous during her time as a Wren, and been removed. Now it turned out that the other one was blocked. She had an operation, in which the tube was blown through. Having your tube blown through conjures up a mental image of something from an Old Master painting, a bright Botticelli angel in a surgical smock setting sexless lips to the reproductive trumpet and sounding the high, true note of fertility. It sounds like an Annunciation under anaesthetic. The reality of the operation was presumably a little different, but she fell pregnant in 1952.

Bill had wanted four sons, for no better reason than that in his Denbighshire childhood he had known a farming family with four sons, which had seemed ideally happy. It didn't occur to him that this family's happiness might have had other sources than brute number and gender of offspring, or indeed that happiness for a farming family may require sons rather than daughters, as it need not for a metropolitan lawyer. He wanted four sons; and so did Sheila.

Babies carry a magnetic charge which can act unpredictably on their carers, and it seems unlikely that Bill and Sheila would have treated daughters with coldness. They maintained a slush pile of tolerable female names, in case: Victoria, Hilary, Zoe. But in the event Sheila bore a son in February 1953, another in October 1954, and a third in November 1957. After that her vindicated ovary rested on its laurels.

The 1950's was not a period in which men attended labour. Bill developed a rather abstract ritual in which he would mark Sheila's confinements by eating out in his favourite restaurant, Leoni's Quo Vadis, extravagantly, and donating a celebratory case of wine to the staff. He could never fully explain why he chose this gesture as against, say, giving something to the nurses in the hospital. But then it was his ritual, not anyone else's, and he didn't really see that there was anything to explain.

Sheila was morbidly afraid that she would drop her first-born, surprised that the nursing home allowed her to take him with her when she left. Shouldn't they have held on to him? They knew what to do. This must be a common fear in first-time mothers, but with Sheila the fear returned only slightly diminished with her second child, and full force with her first grandchild. It seemed that she needed to convince herself every time from scratch that she was not going to drop or break this leaking treasure.

Bill, too, was uneasy holding his children, until they were old enough to play with the boisterousness he enjoyed. His father, Henry, died before the third son was born, but relished bathing the first two, going so far as to tease Bill for his reluctance. But then as a farmer he was used to handling livestock; possibly he was reminded of dipping sheep.

Henry's hands were steady, while Bill's had tremors, tremors both gross and fine, which after he gave up the habit in the 1970's he attributed to his heavy smoking. Sensibly he magnified his vices once they were past, and concluded that his lifestyle was now fine-tuned for longevity. Drink he gave up only for short sprints of abstinence, at health farms in the 1980's.

Early motherhood was the happiest time of Sheila's life, expressed by her in the formula 'I knew what I was supposed to be doing'. From parenthood she had expected no enhancement of self, but that was what she experienced, or at the very least a lifting of conflict.

Her thirties and early forties were lived by Sheila as her prime. She had children and some help with them, au pairs at first foreign and later Welsh, Jutta, Gisela and Ceri – remembered in no particular order as the one who danced on tables, the one who had a pregnancy scare, and the one who married a policeman, and turned out to have been methodically sweeping her cigarette butts under the carpet of her room. Sheila had a successful and devoted husband, who spent much time away but who could be relied upon for a ritually caressive phone call at least once a day.

Soon before the birth of their first child she and Bill moved into No 12, Gray's Inn Square: soon before the birth of their second they moved to a much larger flat opposite, at No 3. Both rents were cushioned by Gray's Inn, which had yet to feel the vulgar necessity of getting the most out of its assets.

Gray's Inn had suffered considerable damage during the war. They were the first tenants of the new No 3, Gray's Inn Square, rebuilt in a paraphrase of the original's Georgian style, and could even modify some of its specifications. So the windowless room at the end of the hall, designated a wine cellar, was instead added on to the sitting-room, making it L-shaped. A cupboard inside the front door was adapted to contain a spiral staircase: the extensive attics thereby made accessible were turned in due course into a children's bedroom, a playroom, a little gym complete with horsehair mats, rings and trapeze, and a further room to accommodate a growing model-railway layout.

This garret, lit only by skylights, was occupied by sons long after Bill and Sheila might have hoped to be free of them, despite the low lintels and the childish beds, two foot six wide, that were the largest that could be carried up the staircase.

Above the attics was the roof, which Sheila could reach up a ladder on sunny days so as to assuage her psoriasis with a tan. On one side the flat overlooked Gray's Inn Walks: Sheila lay in the bath when big with her second child, soon after moving in, and watched sunlight through mature, even overgrown, London planes. On the other side was Gray's Inn Square, also well planted with trees, where babies could be left in their prams with no closer watch kept on them than a mother's casual eye from three floors up.

In those days the ozone layer was as plump as a fresh pillow, though the aerosols that would dent and crease it were already proudly displayed in select bathrooms and kitchens, and sunlight was still considered good for babies. Ten minutes' walk away was Coram's Fields, with playground equipment and a marginally earthier social mix.

Ten minutes' walk in the other direction were Bill's chambers in the Temple, where Sheila's maiden name (under which she had practised) was also on the door. It was possible for her to think of herself as being in the informal sense 'out of practice'. Not that she missed the Bar, and her inglorious career largely devoted to uncontested divorces.

Sheila hadn't practised for long. When novice lawyers stand up in court and speak, they either experience a swelling of chest and voice and brain, an ability to fill the high-ceilinged space with compelling audible logic, or they remain exactly as they were before. She was the second type of lawyer, and realised that she would never know the barrister's joy of being given a red bag to replace her blue one.

This is a ritual recognition by a silk of a junior's outstanding contribution to a significant case, but she knew it was something more: the blue bag changing colour as it leaves the alkaline environment of mediocrity.

She was better suited to law reporting, despite the mad rush to get copy to *The Times* at Printing House Square before five o'clock. She went back to law reporting for a term after the birth of her first son, until she was offered work she could do from home, sub-editing the *Weekly Law Report*. Her work-load could be within reason contracted and expanded. She had passable shorthand, and made her sons' eyes widen, when they were only a little beyond 'The cat sat on the mat', by demonstrating her favourite Pitman hieroglyph, the expert arbitrary squiggle that means *necessary*.

Still, a door-tenant always has a foot in the door, and the door with her name on it was only a short walk away from Gray's Inn. Not that Bill often attempted the walk home from chambers: growing professional success allowed him to indulge the innocent vice of a taxi addiction.

Her lull of fulfilment as a mother allowed Sheila a discreet expansion of personality. After driving the children to school, she would make herself a cup of coffee and sometimes even feel that she deserved it. She was always tense in her pleasures, as if at any moment she might be told she hadn't earned them.

It took her many more years to throw off the conviction, instilled by Lilian, that reading for pleasure by daylight was immoral, and it required some steeling of nerve on her part to read so much as a newspaper before sunset. But she signed up for dance lessons with Bill, who took with surprising agility to that not very Welsh dance, the tango. Only the bossa nova, when that became fashionable, flummoxed them with syncopation.

Sheila had no instinct for housework, but learnt to run a household by a sustained act of will. In the end she was even able to derive a penitential satisfaction from a campaign of spring cleaning waged with the proper fierceness. One legacy of the war years was that she found it very difficult to throw food away, and would hang on to an egg, for instance, if it had the slightest whiff of viability about it. The memory of scarcity carried over into something subtly different: a disbelief in abundance. Far from hoarding supplies, as might be expected from someone who had experienced years of rationing, she never acquired the habit of buying in bulk, preferring to shop every day long after supermarket habits had made inroads into the lives of the middle classes.

Sheila's neighbour and best friend, Cynthia, one of those 'best friends' who savour their differences as much as their similarities, loved running her home and expressed her personality in intensely feminine touches like the collection of little cats on her mantelpiece. Sheila so relaxed in these years that she felt it was legitimate for her too, career woman or no, to collect something ornamental. She decided on bulls rather than cats, not realising that cows outnumber bulls, on the market stalls of the world, by thousands to one. Finding a bull she liked became a challenge in the short term, and a minor annoyance in the long. Finally she changed the rules of her hobby so that anything quadruped and of bovine aspect was admitted.

In her continuing education, which she pursued strongly in these years, Sheila showed both an appetite for knowledge and a strain of masochism. The City Lit (City Literary Institute) was ten minutes' walk away from Gray's Inn, and offered tuition in a huge variety of subjects. Yet over the years Sheila tended to choose classes that would make her feel slightly inadequate – not French conversation but French grammar, not a continuation of long-ago piano lessons but a grounding in harmony and counterpoint. Why brush up on a Chopin prelude when you can be notating a juicy retrograde inversion? She seemed to be seeking a sort of mortification of the intellect by this recurring impulse to take a course too far.

It was as if she needed to prove to her own satisfaction that she wasn't really all that brainy, and consequently that she wasn't wasting herself in the life she had. When she started studying Welsh, she not only set herself to running the gauntlet of that language's notoriously difficult consonantal mutations, but found an area of study where she would always by definition perform less well than the native speaker she had married.

Bill and Sheila and their sons spent the famously idyllic summer of 1959 in Rhosneigr, a village on the west coast of Anglesey. Rhosneigr with its beaches and sunshine seemed to offer an even more propitious setting for the happiness of children than Gray's Inn with its square and its gardens, and the next year Bill used his inheritance from his father, who had died some little time before, to buy a house a little outside the village. The white house he chose (always called The White House, with no presidential irony and no recourse to Welsh) had the great advantage of being separated from the main road by an extensive common, so there was a strict limit on development in the immediate area. Fourteen steps led down to the beach. In September gales, spray would blow from the breakers to strike the kitchen windows with considerable force.

The sea. One day in the early sixties Sheila was swimming with her two older sons, while Bill rolled up the trouser legs of his Prince of Wales check suit to paddle. Suddenly Sheila saw that her boys were swimming out of their depth. As she reached them, she realised that she was barely in her own, and where she put her feet down they met not sand but rock.

She then managed the difficult task of grabbing her children and half swimming, half wading with them to safety. She wanted to alert Bill to a crisis without letting the boys know this was anything but a game. And in fact they had no sense of danger in the water, although they were marked with different memories of the event. One son, looking down, was mesmerised by the sight of Mother's blood swirling thinly from a gash on her leg. The other, looking to shore, was awed by the sight of his father rushing fully clothed into the water. It was only Bill's willingness to endanger his Prince of Wales check suit, and the sodden bank notes from his wallet which dried out slowly on a radiator for the rest of the day, that made the swim seem to contain anything momentous.

If Bill and Sheila collaborated on rescue that day, they were not always so secure in their teamwork. Every generation should have at least one complaint, properly filed and docketed, against the one that went before. That's good form. It prevents bad feeling. The complaint of her sons would have to be that Sheila's hatred of confrontation led her to accept a discrepancy in disciplinary styles.

She didn't punish physically, and Bill did. Bill's punishment normally had the spontaneity that is its excuse or mitigation, but he sometimes fell back into a lawyer's habits. He might cross-examine, looking for inconsistencies, and in the face of denial he would gather evidence. By the time punishment came to be delivered, there was a coldness to it, made worse by his saying, 'This is for hurting your mother,' when the sons knew that if she were there she would extend her mercy.

Between them Bill and Sheila wrote a script by which the male parent acquired a certain vengefulness. Indirectly, therefore, they also shaped their sons' particular versions of the sentence starting 'If I have children I will never ever . . .' and often running to many thousands of clauses, which constitutes the mental life of a teenager. A sentence like the tie-breaking slogan for a newspaper competition.

Sheila's hatred of atmospheres could sometimes prevent her from intervening. Otherwise her life offers no support for a trickle-down theory of trauma. In general the damage done her trickled down only into herself, and wasn't allowed to spill out over others. Is it a characteristic of women as opposed to men, or of the abused as against the respected, that they absorb injuries rather than pass them on as they should? Great abuse, of course, breaks the pattern by exceeding any power to absorb.

In 1969 Bill, after an escalating series of Recorderships (Birkenhead, Swansea, Cardiff), was made a High Court Judge. Such an appointment carries with it a knighthood. Bill glowed with prestige, and talked sweetly to Sheila about having made a Lady of her at long last.

Sheila was wary about having a title, often too shy to include it when asked her name. She was moving now in a world of compliments and stylised attention for which nothing in her background had prepared her. Lilian had not used compliments; she preferred the other weapon. Sheila came to assume that most of the attention she received was either mildly or intensely false, and greeted it with a smile of blankness. One of the things she enjoyed about the winter sports holidays in Austria which the family took at this period was that social life après-ski for once had no connection with legal London and its tortuous skirmishings.

In her forties Sheila undertook two small pieces of editing on herself; she deleted her glasses and she rephrased her nose. She had already tried contact lenses, rather earlier in their technical development, when they covered the entire eyeball and gave those who could tolerate them a permanently startled expression. Sheila had not been one of those who could tolerate them for more than a few minutes at a time, but now that lenses had shrunk to a corneal discreetness she was more successful.

The decision to have an operation on her long-hated nose was mildly unusual in her social circle at that time. But then her motives too were unusual. She wasn't trying to make herself attractive to a new audience, or even an old one. The decision hardly involved other people at all, but it wasn't slackly narcissistic. Sheila was engaged on a rather effective exercise in what would now be called something like self-esteem management. She rid herself of neurosis about her body the way squirrels rid themselves of ticks.

Squirrels, supposedly, pull out a tuft of fur and hold it above their heads while they wade hoppily into a river. It may help to imagine them holding their noses with the other little hand, as the water rises round their heads. Understandably, the ticks swarm upwards on to the decoy tuft. The submerged squirrel then simply flings away the tuft, and regains the safety of the bank. The infestation is over.

Sheila focused her self-hatred on her nose and then flung it away. Her new nose wasn't even quite what she had specified, which had been something jauntily snubby ('tip-tilted' was the word she used), but she had no regrets. The new nose was *not* her nose. That was its virtue and justification. Passing a mirror, she could meet her eyes without rancour.

In May 1973, leaving Moorfields Eye Hospital at the foot of Shaftesbury Avenue, where she had been doing voluntary work, Sheila made a small dent in a Ford Transit van. The van made a much larger dent in her.

It was a rainy day, with a wind, and Sheila may have held her umbrella in such a way that she could not see the approach of the van, released from the traffic lights nearby and bounding towards her. She was certainly much preoccupied at that time with the fate of her best friend, Cynthia, who was suffering from a bone disease. These contributory factors have to be reconstituted artificially, since she had no memory of being struck. Like her despair at sea, these were some of the many moments that go missing from a life: missing but immense, the amnesias of ecstasy and accident.

An ambulance was called, to take her to the Middlesex Hospital not far off. Sheila was alert enough to give a name when asked for one, but not quite alert enough to give the right one. The name she gave seems to have belonged to the last person she talked to, during her morning stint of wheeling round the trolley of cassette players and books on tape.

At the hospital, she was booked in under the name she had given, and was X-rayed. No one, however, looked with any attention at the resulting plates, so it was not noticed that she had suffered a comminuted fracture at the base of the skull.

'Comminuted' is posh for 'like a little jigsaw'. There was only one superficial injury, to the scalp, so they sewed that up. In the process they sewed hair into the wound, which subsequently became infected.

Of all the professionals through whose hands she passed that afternoon, it is only the ambulance men who emerge with any credit as diagnosticians. They at least realised that this was a woman who wouldn't be in good shape any time soon, and wouldn't be asking any awkward questions about the disappearance of her ear-rings.

Sheila's medical problems didn't end with the little jigsaw of skull fractures. There was also the question of the contrecoup injury. The brain suffers when a sharp blow causes it to strike the side of the skull away from the impact. The brain suffers.

Sheila's first bit of good luck that day was that an acquaintance, who had also done some voluntary work at Moorfields, was told by the staff there that her friend had been knocked down and was now in the Middlesex. Someone therefore turned up at the hospital who was able to clear up the question of the name, and also to sit with Sheila long enough to realise that she wasn't merely shocked and confused but seriously ill. The pressure of blood in her brain was building up to a dangerous extent, and she was beginning to have small stroke-like seizures on one side of her body.

From this point on, her luck changed abruptly. At last the X-rays were looked at properly, and John Firth, a brain surgeon with an experimental technique, was alerted for duty. Messages could finally be sent to Bill in court in Cardiff, and relayed by him to the sons, at their various educational establishments.

John Firth operated for five hours. He was a good surgeon, so good in fact that he dreamt of something better, and subsequently stood for the constituency of Orkney in Parliament.

He had already started operating by the time any family member was able to attend. The technique he used involved removing an area of bone and refrigerating it for later reinsertion. In the meantime the brain would be able to expand after its trauma, and if there was a complication there would be no need to cut healing bone all over again. From the point of view of an era of keyhole surgery, this seems more like barn-door surgery, but it was the state of the art in its day. One of the first things Bill was told by John Firth, when he arrived, was that this was a good time to have a neglected comminuted fracture of the skull and consequent subdural haemorrhage. A few years ago there would have been no hope, and he had used a new ventilation technique which allowed him to operate for longer, and so be more thorough.

Even so, he wasn't exactly optimistic – to the extent that anyone wearing rubber gloves stained with the blood of a man's wife can communicate optimism to him. Sheila might recover physical mobility and mental power; she might lose either, or both.

In fact her recovery was good. Her first gesture on regaining consciousness, even before she had taken in what exactly had happened to her, was to reach a hand up to her nose. It was safe, it was still there; the new improved nose, the nose she could live with. Only then did her hand go further up, to explore the alien headdress of the plaster cast that now protected her skull.

The trap-door of bone from her head was kept in a fridge

for six weeks. She was told about it in terms of a tennis-ball. Bill told her that a piece of bone the size of a tennis-ball had been removed. A tennis-ball, a rough sphere. Had they taken some brain as well? It was confusing, it wasn't reassuring, this domesticating description of what was gone from her head.

But then we make clumsy assessments of the size of delinquent body parts. If it isn't sport it's fruit – it's always either sport or fruit. Of swollen testicles or sinister growths, we say that they're the size of a tennis-ball, or the size of a football. The size of an orange, the size of a grapefruit. Pathologists perhaps sometimes see things they compare to watermelons or medicine balls.

What Bill meant was that the piece of skull that went missing from Sheila's head, and was then reunited with it, was the size of a flattish section of a tennis-ball, or the *slice* of an orange. In a separate operation, the little area of bone that had gone septic after hair was sewn into her wound was cut out. The size of a marble, the size of a cherry.

In a way, when she reached her hand up that first waking day in hospital and met the firm reassuring prow of her chosen nose, what she felt was a mirage. In a manner of speaking, her nose was missing, and didn't come back. Sometimes it seemed that doctors could do anything these days, that they could open an inspection hatch in the brain and knot the dangling wires together, but they couldn't bring her nose back. They couldn't do that. Her nose was dead, or at best in a coma.

Whether because the sensing fibres had been flattened by the van's impact, or because the area of the brain that interpreted their signals had been closed down while the blood pressure built up unnoticed, Sheila never smelt anything again, not fresh bread nor burning hair. The technical term for this is anosmia. Strange: loss of sight or hearing is privileged with an Anglo-Saxon term, while loss of smell remains in Greek, as if this is a rather fancy deprivation. Never mind that smell is the most basic sense, the one that crouches lowest in the brain.

Her sense of smell was the only absolute loss from the accident, and a good bargain by any standards, compared with how her prospects were announced on the night of the operation. She had sustained damage to the trigeminal nerve that runs down the side of the face, and it was a long time before the neural frazzling settled down, giving her relief from adjacent areas of numbness and a tingly distorted sensitivity.

Her hair grew back from its pre-operative shearing, though less curly than before and perhaps less full – but then few women of fifty (an age she reached a few months after the accident) are natural casting for Rapunzel. She had kept the shape of her chosen nose, losing only its function. Yet loss of nasal function is not nothing.

The structural logic of perception dictates that if you are nose-blind, nose-deaf, then you are palate-impaired, 'hard of tasting' as people are said to be hard of hearing. You may sense only the basic categories of taste as they are exemplified by what is actually in your mouth. What happens on your palate is no longer vivid dinner, but your taste-buds attempting a slightly muzzy after-dinner game, a round of charades. Spice or condiment, two syllables, let's see, must be garlic. Ginger?

You may have a sort of speckled insensitivity, able to detect some subtle flavours, defeated by ones which your fellow-diners pronounce strong. Texture in food tends to become more important in this domain of straitened sensation, celery's crunch being less elusive than its tang. If you have weight to spare, you will tend to lose it: having your jaws wired is a clumsy procedure compared to having the wiring of your nose disconnected. Without the flaring alarms of the nostrils sending any signals, you will have to remind yourself to eat, and if you are slim, like Sheila, you must guard against unhealthy weight-loss.

This was a period in which brain surgeons were just beginning, while talking to relatives of those on whom they had operated, tentatively to invoke comparisons with computers. In 1973, when even a major hospital such as the Middlesex had no great investment in hardware, and private individuals were even less familiar with the subject, to say that a brain was like a computer was to make a rather abstract statement, but at least it might convey the information that an injured brain heals differently from a broken leg. Bill was told that with luck Sheila, though technically brain-damaged, would retain her skills and her memories. Important 'files' of memory in damaged tissue would somehow be transcribed, in the weeks to come, on to fresh pages of the mind. The word 'file' sounded old-fashioned, even bureaucratic; it had yet to take on a modern overtone. It suggested tall cabinets of olive-green metal.

It was likely that Sheila's short-term memory would be impaired – the idea seemed to be that it would get squeezed out by the demands of all that transcription – though the prognosis overall was remarkably good.

Sheila gingerly took the morning sunlight in the little hidden garden of the hospital. During those early days and early nights, dozing or solidly asleep, Sheila was visited by marvel-

lously humdrum dreams. She dreamt entire days of inconse-
quence, from morning tea to evening toothbrush, while her
brain absorbed the fact of damage.

The transcription was certainly accomplished, but there
were perhaps hidden costs. Sheila was bound to feel more
anxious about her mental quickness. No one to whom the
label of 'brain damage' has been attached will venture into
conversation without subliminal hesitation: am I talking sense,
am I even using language? Perhaps I'm talking in numbers,
and people are only pretending to understand out of polite-
ness, or for their own reasons.

After 1973, Sheila became unduly anxious about the pro-
nunciation of disputed words, words like 'controversy',
'decade' or indeed 'dispute'. At moments of trivial stress she
would run out of words altogether and resort to a small hand-
ful of coinages, so that 'I've spilt a bit of wine on the carpet'
came out 'I've spoobed a bit on the doo-dah-day'.

She had never had much taste for the sort of film or play
that keeps you guessing, for suspense of any ambitious kind,
but after 1973 indifference turned to positive aversion. All it
took was one plot twist or unexplained development and she
would defensively withdraw her attention, convinced that in
her stupidity she had missed something vital which would
make the entire plot clear to everyone else in the world.

She found it harder to make decisions, particularly about
trivial questions. She would spend what felt like absurd
amounts of time deadlocked about stupid things, like what to
prepare for dinner, as if a marble in her mind was going round
and round, never able to settle in the slot marked 'Chop' or
'Fish'.

The experience of denting a Ford Transit van, and being dented in her turn, wrenched Sheila out of her generation. It foreshortened her sense of priorities, so that she found anything short of physical trauma relatively hard to get worked up about. For this reason she became a more indulgent parent. Let them smoke, let them fool around, so long as they look both ways before they cross the road: that was more or less her attitude. Yet survival also made her feel worthless.

Cynthia's illness didn't let up. She and her husband and son came to stay in Anglesey during the summer after the accident. Sheila insisted on being ready for this, but it couldn't be anything but a strain on her, even before Cynthia walked unseeing into a sliding glass door and broke one of the glass bones in her arm. She was taken to the Caernarvon and Anglesey Hospital, the C and A, known locally (alas) as the 'Cremations and Amputations', where the bell-pull by her bed intended to summon the nurses made no sound.

Later that summer Sheila, out walking with Bill in Rhosneigr village and despairing of expressing her feelings of inadequacy, knowing that it was terrible ingratitude for recipients of miraculous reprieves from death or brain-death not to love their lives, broke away from him and tried to throw herself in front of a car. She discovered that road accidents don't always come when they're called, any more than children do. The car was going at no great pace, and swerved without even coming close. Sheila ran down to the beach, but Bill followed after her and in due course they returned together to the house.

It was medically suggested that what Sheila's brain needed, to shake it out of the depression that seemed to have followed from so much transcription, was a course of electric shock treatment. Obediently she paid weekly visits to Queen Square, where the attempt was made to expel her low feelings with high voltage. The theory of ECT is simply stated: there isn't one. It is only a practice, one devised to capitalise on a discovery made in the 1940's, that epileptics don't get depressed. Depressives, therefore, should be enabled to reap the benefits of epilepsy. Counterfeit fits were provoked originally by means of saline injections, before the superiority of electricity was established.

Sheila would come to herself piecemeal, in fuzzy instalments, and would make efforts to leave without an escort, though Bill or a son was invariably on the way to pick her up. Having her brain struck by tame lightning had the temporary effect of simplifying her mental operations, so that she had no idea, when she came round, that she was the sort of person that people looked after and cared for.

On the other hand her mind, even at its most smooth-running, had trouble entertaining such a cosy idea. This was in fact precisely the state of affairs that electro-convulsive therapy was in some way supposed to remedy.

ECT was a mixed success at best. Since it further scrambled Sheila's short-term memory over the period of the treatment, she could never know whether to believe Bill's assurances that she was getting better week by week, shock by shock. She didn't have much to go on. She knew her husband well enough to understand that he liked problems that could be solved quickly, and depressives who could be cheered up with a single dose of his energy. He didn't enjoy being patient, except for short bursts, and her misery would end up undermining and exasperating him.

Cynthia Terry died in 1974, and in so doing fixed the certainty in Sheila's mind that the wrong woman had survived. Hadn't Cynthia loved life, as Sheila never quite managed to do? Sheila spent increasing amounts of mental time in a sort of agonising parallel universe, in which Cynthia stoutly recovered, while Bill in due time put aside his bereavement and married a Nice Ordinary Woman, who was good to Sheila's sons.

Thinking about the world better off without her, following through into the future her fantasy of family life soothed by her death, was both a temptation and a torture, an addiction. A perversion.

Only someone with a strong streak of self-abasement, a chronically lowered sense of self, could have wished on her children that thing from which she had so much suffered, a stepmother.

It was during this period that Sheila remarked to her least effusive son that she was glad *he* at least wasn't a sentimentalist, and would turn off her life-support system without a second thought. She was quite taken aback when he reacted with dismay. There was no irony intended: she had meant it as a compliment.

If this was a time of interior collapse, it was also somehow a time of self-reconstruction. Sheila put into action a plan that predated her accident, and applied to be the chairman of a rent-assessment panel. Her legal background qualified her for the job, which would be part-time – two days a week, say, plus the appropriate preparation. It was also a whole new area of work, with every possibility of the slowness and confusion she found in herself, her general inadequacy confirmed by the accident, being shown up. Perhaps it was best to know for sure, one way or the other.

Partly, too, she was urged on by irritation. If one more Gray's Inn acquaintance told her she was marvellous to have made such a recovery she was sure she would scream. What sort of achievement was it to come back from the dead, if all you were going to do with your ransomed life was sit around at idiot tea parties chattering about the marvels of modern science? She should go in for this ambitious new job, fall flat on her face and become properly acquainted with failure. Get it over with.

In fact she was a quietly spectacular success in the role. Her legal qualifications were indispensable, but what the job chiefly called for was patience and tact. The diffidence of Sheila's authority was underpinned by the fact that, after the accident, she was never altogether convinced of the accuracy of her arithmetic or her reading of the law. She was always open to correction or second thoughts.

The panel's offices were in Newlands House, just across Mortimer Street, as it happens, from the Middlesex Hospital. The recovery that had got under way at the Middlesex, after its false start, was furthered by the bureaucracy on the other side of the street.

Sheila would be asked some weeks in advance whether she was free to work on a particular day, so she had a certain amount of control over her schedule. Successive Rent Acts narrowed the purview of the panel, and Sheila sometimes had the feeling of being a smiling irrelevance. Nevertheless she enjoyed the work, with its starchy camaraderie: the duties expected of the chairman included buying drinks for the other panel members in a pub at lunchtime. The real rare pleasure of the job was being allowed into people's homes and being warmly invited to inspect them, having people point out defects or improvements with a touching frankness and deference.

Every now and then a rent-assessment panel was called upon to inspect premises occupied by someone self-neglecting or demented. On those occasions Sheila's mild poise was much remarked on by her fellow members. No degree of disarray in living quarters shook her. No stench seemed able to make an impact. They complimented her on the seamlessness of her self-control, while she permitted herself a faint anosmic smile.

In the private life of her anosmia, Sheila didn't give up the use of perfume. She was unwilling to do without the rituals of fragrance, reassurance that goes beyond the sensual. She successfully controlled the impulse to anoint herself more freely – the delusion that an extinct faculty might somehow be triggered by sheer excess of stimulus.

Still, she had a sense of frustration whenever a new perfume was launched. She didn't want to be trapped in the past by the subtle feminine carbon-dating of scent, stubbornly attached to her old faithfuls, Balmain's Vent Vert, Guerlain's Chant d'Arôme, when everyone else had moved on. A new advertising campaign would quicken her mental nostrils and make her curious, unless it was for an obviously inappropriate scent, something sultry or saccharine.

Sometimes she would buy the smallest possible bottle of something announced as fresh or citric, dab a tiny bit on, and then do what women without daughters or female intimates must do. Ask a man.

The men in her family would try with their snuffling male noses and their small vocabularies of sensation to inform her. Bill would say she smelt wonderful, but then he always said that, and his marriage-long inability to spot a new item of clothing unless it was pulled out of a smart carrier bag made him a suspect witness. Her boys were little better, struggling to be honest but baffled by even elementary principles of perfumery: that essences smell differently on different skins, that treble notes evanesce and bass ones linger.

The boys were more reliable when she held a vest or a pair of Bill's socks under their noses and asked whether these items needed washing. The doggy binary of fresh against stinky: *that* they could manage.

So why did she never have second thoughts about the son-heaviness of her family? The sonniness of Bill's temperament at least has a story to back it up – the fable of the four happy farming brothers. Sheila's falling in with the fable has no story of its own. And wouldn't it have been nice for her, if not at first then later, to have a gender ally in the home?

The only obvious possibility – and it is *thoroughly* obvious, as flat and pat as a newspaper think-piece – is that historically it was women who had damaged Sheila, Gladys by desertion, Lilian by imposition. It was men, historically, who had rescued her: Xavier Cremades (toast him in many tiny sherries), John Firth (toast him in tumblers of Scotch). Even, somehow, the toastmaster himself. Even Bill.

Bill was proud of Sheila's recovery, and liked to invite her down to Judges' Lodgings to show her off. Sheila didn't mind too much, except when she cancelled an evening class, took a train down to Bodmin or Norwich or Carlisle, and then had to sit at the dinner table and listen to Bill saying how wonderfully clever she was, how she was always studying something arty, linguistic or musical, if not all three.

Sheila received a lot of complimentary attention at these dinners, as on most formal occasions, but she had long since learnt to neutralise it mentally. She reasoned that in an Ancient and Honourable Society like Gray's Inn, so closely tied to a hierarchical profession, deference was poured so freely over a High Court Judge that some of it slopped on to his lady wife – just as tea sometimes spills from teacup to saucer. Bill lapped it up, but she felt she knew better. Nothing she heard was actually about her.

As a wife she realised that she had an obligation to be a good sport on these occasions, and didn't mind putting on the glad rags once in a while. She would even have her hair done, something she hated, before she left London. She was convinced that she had virtually no hair left, just as anorexic teenagers imagine themselves saddled with jodhpurs of cellulite. Sheila was a trichological anorexic, a trichorexic. She couldn't bear to see her hair in the mirror. If ever she mentioned her fears to Bill, of course, he only talked about his mother and her bloody Transformation. He seemed to be making out that what she feared was in some way a test of character – as if she needed any more of those. Something she wasn't allowed to mind.

There weren't all that many consolations of later life, or so Sheila found, but one unexpected one was that you could dress entirely for your own pleasure, now that nobody minded one way or the other. She liked the style of dress required by her work, which she interpreted as being *crisp* but not *cold*. It was no great effort to combine black and white, clean lines and the occasional flirty detail, so as to end up with ensembles that were professional but not unfriendly.

Even when she wasn't working she gravitated towards a style of dress that was somewhere between formal and informal. She favoured some third state between rigour and casualness, something neither chilly nor gushy. She had never suited either flatties or stilettos – for her it must always be a medium heel. Her clothes were never meant to intimidate anyone, but they played their part in helping her to stay in control of herself, whatever she felt like really.

The passing of time had not made her repent of the principles of dress she had laid down for herself as a young woman:

1. Navy makes my face look muddy.

2. I have Joan Crawford shoulders, so pads of any kind make me look as if I've forgotten to take the coat-hanger out of my jacket.

3. My knees are vile and not to be seen by strangers.

After psoriasis came along, elbows were added to the knee embargo. Nobody else ever noticed the Joan Crawford shoulders, which proved to Sheila's satisfaction that she had learnt how to draw attention away from them. She'd learnt a thing or two.

There was never an item of clothing in the shops that she wanted as much as she had wanted a little gingham skirt she'd seen in a shop-window after the war, blue with contrasting pockets, one red, one green, when she didn't have the necessary coupons. Otherwise she managed pretty well.

Sheila was brave enough to resume working for Moorfields

on Monday mornings, despite the painful associations with her past, her personal Accident Black Spot invisibly marked on the road metal. In the late seventies the Shaftesbury Avenue branch of the hospital closed down, and Sheila volunteered at Old Street instead.

Indefatigably she pushed the trolley of talking books, trying to wean people off trash, in an interlude of blindness that might even be merciful in this respect, without directly refusing them what they wanted. So if someone asked for a romance, Sheila would think, well, quite a lot of books are romances when you think about it. Surely listening to *Rebecca* had to be more enjoyable than the tired old clip-clop of something from the Cartland stable?

Her slimness, and the vigour with which she pushed the trolley, deceived some of the patients into thinking they were being served by a much younger woman. Sensing a lithe displacement of air, men would inhale appreciatively, and be greeted by a fresh and citric scent, difficult to place.

Sheila's flexibility and energy were notable – but then her Aunt Dot, at that time in her nineties, was proud of her sit-ups. Aunt Dot had been a dance teacher; she couldn't walk, but she could do sit-ups. Sheila went ice-skating regularly, at Queens Club in Queensway, at long last conquering her instinctive fear of going backwards on the ice. On summer holidays in Anglesey, she remained the family's water-skiing star, even getting the knack of the monoski.

She could have gone on water-skiing for hours, if it wasn't for the numbness in her fingers. All her life her extremities had been susceptible to cold, so that her fingers went white when she so much as washed a summer salad. Her system had no sense of proportion. It would interpret a sinkful of lettuce and tomatoes as the leading edge of an arctic tempest, requiring emergency measures, the hoarding of blood near the heart.

The principal indignity of the menopause, from her point of view, was having hot flushes that did nothing to warm her fingers and toes. At work, when there were inspections to be done in weather that was less than balmy, she learnt to use a little hand-warmer bought from a camping and survival shop. A tablet ignited at the beginning of the working day and laid carefully inside the little case would keep her hands functioning for hours. If the tablet ran out, on the other hand, she would have to spend ages bringing her fingers agonisingly back to life in warm water.

Eventually the tendency to numbness was diagnosed as Raynaud's Phenomenon, giving Sheila another support-group publication to subscribe to, along with the anguished bulletins from Compassion in World Farming and the encouraging updates in her psoriasis newsletter. Psoriasis was beginning to yield to science over this period, first to PUVA, a combination of sensitising pill and sun-ray lamp, and finally to the drug methotrexate, despite its whispered carcinogenic reputation. Sheila could adjust the dosage to keep lesions at bay.

Science was slower in getting to grips with depression. Whatever medication she was taking during these years, there was a part of Sheila that permanently identified with the abused calves shown in the Compassion in World Farming literature. Seeing herself as veal, atrociously blanched and tender.

While Bill lived in the present, almost to a fault, supremely confident that he was making provision for the years ahead,

Sheila lived in the most dismal of futures, imagining eventu-
alities that she felt she could do nothing to prevent. More than
ever she felt there was a stroke in her head, waiting to pounce,
and knowing her luck she'd hang on for years, unable to
speak, trying to close her lopsided mouth round a soup-
spoon.

At the same time, her mind ran obsessively over the past,
telling her that she had started with a good hand of cards but
had somehow thrown them all away, letting all her advantages
come to nothing. The fault was not in the deal but in the play.
If she could only think her way back to the exact point where
she had gone wrong, she could . . . what? She would know,
that was all, and perhaps she'd be able to live with the knowledge. She reached back mentally into the past, beyond the
accident, as far as Lilian, but she could never quite fix the
moment of failure.

The house in Anglesey, associated though it was with the
heyday of motherhood, was becoming a problem and a burden. Sheila's sons gave no hint of reproductive ambition, and
it wasn't that she was in any hurry to be a grandmother. But
the logic of a holiday home by the sea fell down if there was-
n't a breeding population of Mars-Joneses, a supply of small
people to furnish the place appropriately with laughter and
abandoned sandy swimsuits. She was afraid of the White
House becoming a white elephant.

Already there were times when she and Bill were there
alone, and she looked with a sinking feeling from the chop on
her dinner plate to the chop on his. How was it possible to
have a sinking feeling when your feelings were a sink in the
first place? She felt she was getting not a holiday but a

prophecy of retirement. She noticed that sons visited not casually, spontaneously, but in pairs. Their visits had become dutiful, and perhaps there was even a system in operation, of coordinating phone calls to make sure that no son was ever there on his own with those uninteresting people, parents.

She told Bill that she didn't want to retire to Anglesey. He didn't disagree – out of season the island could be bleak – but Sheila wasn't able to make any positive suggestion about the years to come. It was retirement itself she dreaded, the dreary horror of her future.

In 1981 the decision was made to sell the White House, though to the extent that the debate over the house had been a debate about how to handle retirement, no progress had been made. Still, holidays for Sheila (on cruise ships to warm places with ruins and lectures) were now authentic exemptions from running a house, and that was certainly an improvement.

Bill invested the proceeds of the sale in stocks and shares, but in captivity the money could not be persuaded to breed, and slowly pined away. The market collapse in 1987 was only the clincher, after which the money lay on its back in the cage, stiff paws in the air.

A curious feature of Sheila's depression had always been that it contained no element of lethargy. She had plenty of energy, but it brought her no satisfaction. She was very struck by the term 'anhedonia', meaning the inability to experience pleasure, when she read that this had been the original title of the film *Annie Hall*, and determined to memorise it. From the time that she had been told that the learning of new words was the hardest task she could impose on a traumatised brain, she had become something of a bulimic of vocabulary.

How to combat anhedonia? One idea was to go to a therapist, specifically a Jungian, since this school of psychology
seemed less obsessed with damage than most. She was
estranged from her own vitality, that was what was the matter
with her, and being united with your own vitality sounded
like an orthodox Jungian goal. In practice, though, the sessions yielded little, and if her therapist was at one with his
vitality he did a good job of concealing it.

Perhaps the mind and spirit could be reached through the
body? She enrolled in a yoga class, feeling that she should take
advantage of a flexibility unusual in a sixty-year-old. She had
no difficulty with the exercises, but found the experience
anything but transcendent. One particular thing she found
unable to transcend was the fear that the individual mats used
in the class, sometimes warm and damp from a previous session, were actively smelly. Not being able to verify her
suspicions directly, and having an anosmic's natural horror of
the undetectably unclean, she felt more than ever entrapped in
her body and her negative emotions.

Early in 1985 Sheila realised that she had unaccountably
fallen behind in her programme of screening for breast cancer.
She was months late, and when she duly arranged an appointment a lump was announced. She agreed to surgery, which
revealed that the lump had indeed been a novice malignancy.

The men around her, simple souls, argued that if she really
wanted to be dead she would hardly have taken measures,
however belated, to preserve herself. But Sheila was not so
easily to be tricked into manifesting a life-wish. She knew
perfectly well she would survive, worse luck, she just didn't

want to be any more maimed than could be helped. Health was a lottery, and she was only interested in the jackpot. Nothing else would do.

Her life was no more than an old plate for her, but if she was going to be denied the satisfaction of going properly smash, she would choose to have the smallest possible number of cracks.

The surgery was successful, and the disfigurement insignificant. She found she didn't think about it. Again, she had a short-term preoccupation, as she had had in the Middlesex in 1973, when she had reached for her hard-won nose. Would she be able to continue taking methotrexate, or would psoriasis start to win all over again? That was what she wanted to know.

In the event there was no objection, as long as she continued with regular liver biopsies. She was punctilious with these appointments, at least, and never missed one.

If Sheila had few expectations of motherhood, she had none of grandmotherhood. It was only another form of retirement, really, a genetic redundancy notice. Yet when it came she took a pleasure in it that became, in time, intense. At last the family's notional Welshness came in handy: Sheila was called Nain (pronounced Nine), Bill Taid (Tide), and these toddler-friendly monosyllables gave them an automatic advantage over Grandmothers and Grandfathers. Gray's Inn Walks proved an undiminished asset, and the playground in Coram's Fields re-emerged as a resource after thirty years. There was even some new equipment.

When she retired from the rent-assessment panel, after twenty years, she was given a party – something that even

Sheila couldn't quite dismiss as an empty gesture, since no retiring chairman in her time had been honoured in this way.

Bill had retired in 1990, with an agenda of virtually torrential self-expression: he would perfect his neglected guitar-playing, memoirs and plays would pour from him. He had the titles ready. When a couple of years down the line Sheila shyly enquired what had become of all the creativity, he replied that he was catching up on a backlog that had built up during those long and stressful years at the Bar and on the bench. This as he explained it was a backlog of idleness, and would take an indefinite time to clear up.

He had remained in harness as long as he could, which means seventy-five in the case of High Court Judges, so perhaps he too was dreading retirement, though he was not a man who could be made to own up to dreading anything, on either side of the grave.

Husband and wife had in common a religious background, but Bill was the one with the religious conviction, though he called it, unembarrassed, blind faith. He never seemed to pray, and was less than fanatical about church attendance. There were services in Gray's Inn chapel during the short legal terms, and the Mars-Joneses usually attended, but there was a social element involved (seating was hierarchical, with designated places for Benchers, members of the Inn's governing body, and their spouses) and even a nutritional one, since lunch was laid on afterwards in Hall.

When there were children to be brought up, Bill and Sheila attended the City Temple in Holborn Viaduct, which was somewhat in the grain of Bill's native Congregationalism, but after the glory days of Dr Weatherhead and then Kenneth

Slack things became a bit evangelical, and they discontinued the habit in the 1980's.

Sheila would often attend early-morning Communion in Gray's Inn, a sacrament poorly timed to attract Bill, but she was never impressed with the purity of her own heart, before or after Eucharist. Her motivations seemed to her in general horribly self-serving, and she would brood guiltily over sharp replies to testy questions which Bill had long since forgotten asking.

Sheila had more doubts than convictions, religiously, but could not go to bed without spending time on her knees, praying. She was unable to pray in any other position. But then it was the same with teeth: Bill rarely brushed but expected dental salvation, while Sheila wrestled nightly with floss, though her teeth were too closely set to allow it easy access, and lived in fear of the hell of dentures.

There was no retirement age for helpers at Moorfields, thank God, and there was also the possibility of new voluntary work. Sheila offered her services (and the benefit of her legal training) to a charitable organisation called Access to Justice, conveniently located in High Holborn. Which got her out of the house another half-day a week.

Over the years, Sheila's discreet death-wish held out against a whole series of medication regimes. When her GP asked her how she was, she would find herself saying she was all right. It saved trouble, and one of the words she had committed to memory after the accident – 'endogenous', as applied to her type of depression – made her think that medication wasn't really going to make a difference. She took the pills obedi-ently, though sometimes when she felt woolly she would taper down the doses, until she reached the point of wanting nothing better than to feel woolly again.

She wasn't melodramatic about wanting to be dead, and she normally knew better than to blurt it out. Whenever she particularly liked a piece of music, she would say that she wanted it played at her funeral, but that was as far as it went, and she smiled when it was pointed out to her that her funeral was turning into a music festival lasting many days.

Still, in the early nineties, when she was explaining why she had an irrational resistance to selling the car, she let something slip. Bill's decreasing mobility made taxis much more practical, after all. She could see the logic. Finally she admitted the basis of her affection for the vehicle. She had made the decision to keep Bill company while he was alive, but after that she was a free woman, and she was reasonably sure she could do the job with the car. She had no faith in pills, one way or the other.

The moment she had spoken she regretted the bafflement and pain she had caused, and guilt made her agree to see the doctor again. She managed to seem reasonably enthusiastic, even, doing her mime of hope, and this time, out of family loyalty, she didn't say she felt all right when the doctor asked how she was.

Once she came close to having her bluff called, when a son brought her a form of paper called a Living Will and suggested that she fill it in – if she was really so concerned about the possibility of being internally pulped by a stroke, but left living. It was a perfectly sensible suggestion, but then she lost the form in the flood tide of Bill's accumulated papers: financial reports, betting advice, wartime letters mysteriously resurrected from the filing cabinet, and despairing appeals from the *Reader's Digest* for payment regarding gardening books Bill denied ever having ordered. After that, she thought it would be kinder not to ask for another copy of the form; bad enough to be meekly suicidal without being vague as well.

If this made her seem insincere in her contemplation of last things, then that was just too bad. She was having to contemplate the possibility that she truly was a thing she did not admire, came close to despising: a survivor. To be a survivor was not an identity. It showed something close to bad taste, like being the last person to leave a party, when you were no particular friend of the host.

She had slim hopes of predeceasing Bill. The closest thing she had to true self-destructive behaviour was her continuing cigarette habit, but her consumption of tobacco had risen and fallen in a bell curve across the decades since the days when smoking had been an aromatic declaration of independence. After her accident might have been a sensible time to stop, except that those who lose their sense of smell forfeit one of the positive motivations for kicking the habit. Carrying on with her smoking was one of the few faintly defiant aspects of her recovery.

By the early nineties she was down to three Silk Cut Extra Mild a day. It was less of a crime against herself than a homoeopathic tincture of nicotine. Sons would tease her by telling her not to forget to smoke. Saying goodnight, they would remind her that she still had one cigarette to get through before bedtime, to be sure not to skip it.

When she gave up at last, she was spared the dismal fate of

being a person without vices by a sudden passion for plain
chocolate digestive biscuits. Her most recent anti-depressant
medication increased her appetite across the board, but this
was different. It was the first time she had actively craved
something sweet since her childhood love affair with treacle
tart. She described her taste for the odd chocky bicky in
terms of compulsive behaviour, as if she'd be throwing herself
down the staircase of Kensington Palace next.

If this was a binge, it was a binge in extreme slow motion,
impossible to spot amid the entrenched moderation of her
habits. She showed no signs of swelling back up from her
wiry size 8 (6 or even smaller in the puzzlingly inflated
American sizing) to the buxom size 12 she had been the day
she married.

This after all was a woman with a passion for strong cheddar
who for years restricted herself to the placebo cheese Edam,
and that in small quantities, for fear of elevating her level of
cholesterol. Perhaps the austere binge on biscuits was only a letting up of anhedonia in one particular area, a reacquaintance
with the basics of pleasure as pleasure-lovers experience it.

Sheila's vision had clouded over during the eighties, to the
point where actors were fuzzy angels even from the front
stalls of a theatre. She was told that she could have her
cataracts removed more or less when she wanted, but she
chose to wait until after retirement. She couldn't bear to give
up even a day of work while she was still entitled to it. That
way, too, she would have one thing to look forward to after
being put out to grass. She would be able to see in full, crisp
detail the dreary paddock of her life.

There was a bad moment, during one operation, when

she felt a flat click inside her head and heard the laser opera-
tor swear quietly to himself. He'd cracked the new lens that he
was meant to be bonding into place. In the end, though, her
vision settled down without any more surgery. She now had
one eye calibrated for vision at a distance, the other one for
close work, a bizarre-sounding arrangement when first it was
put to her but perfectly practicable. For the first time since she
was a child she was wearing neither glasses nor contacts, and
she could not only watch the play but read the programme. It
wasn't the perfect sight without glasses promised so long ago
by that charlatan Bates, but it was good enough.

Difficult to pass up such an image of bifocal awareness,
vision not perfect but adequate for objects both near and far.
To take stock: Sheila in her seventies is a woman defined as
depressive but tirelessly energetic. Only now has she given in
to the practicality of a shopping trolley on her daily trips to
Leather Lane. At last she makes that concession to the icon-
ography of mumsiness, as she trots on narrow feet daily to the
shops, to buy the robust cheese she now allows herself, for the
Mocha Italia coffee from the Continental Stores that reliably
stings her palate.

If depressives were electronically tagged like criminals so
that their doctors could better monitor their progress, it
would seem to the tracking team that Sheila had mischiev-
ously passed off her tag on some very purposeful little person,
someone who surges indomitably to the theatre, to
Moorfields, to the Royal Academy or the Tate, to Coram's
Fields, to Access to Justice. Depression in her case seems to be
more a matter of energy frustrated than killed, energy
ingrown like a toenail.

Playing with her grandchildren, a group in which the girls now outnumber the boys without any slackening in her interest, she seems absurdly spry. Uncoiling from a long-maintained crouch in the wardrobe where a four-year-old has failed to find her, she mimes a wince at the crepitus of her knees, and seems more than ever like a mediocre actress remembering she has been cast as an old woman. Indulging in a little stage business. It is a poor impersonation of a London senior citizen in the twentieth century.

Sheila has her hair tinted out of a sense of aesthetic preference rather than vanity, if that distinction is tenable, saying she'd be happy to go white but can't abide dirty grey. She sits by the telephone in the sitting-room of No 3, Gray's Inn Square, reading a novel boldly by daylight, but jumps infallibly whenever it rings (the phone, not the novel). From the fierceness of her reaction you would think that Alexander Graham Bell had only just invented the instrument. That he had installed the prototype in Sheila's sitting-room, so as to start it up every now and then, to see if it worked.

Sheila's life has been rich as well as, for long periods, almost continuously unhappy, although the richness of it is not apparent to her. She has felt trapped, first by other people's choices and then by her own. Like any animal in a trap, she has gnawed at her own leg to get free – it's just that sometimes she has gnawed the wrong leg.

Every so often, her life has run into a wall, the wall of a separation (from a mother, a father, a floating husband, a nose, a job) or a collision (with a stepmother or a Ford Transit). Is it surprising that when a life runs into a wall it is changed? Not surprising. The surprising thing is actually the reverse:

how much people bring, stuffed into their pockets, clenched between their teeth, over the wall and into the after life.

When Sheila married, she knew that sooner or later, Bill's nature being what it was, she would have to cough up children. That was always the phrasing she used, to 'cough them up'. She gave birth to Tim in 1953, Adam in 1954 and Matthew in 1957. I am the middle cough of her womb's coughing fit from the 1950's. I love my life, which isn't quite the same as saying that I expect happiness from it. One of Sheila's virtues as a mother was to have stopped telling us, quite early on, that everything was going to be all right.

T his
C r y i n g - T h i n g

K ATE   S AUNDERS

Kate Saunders was born in London. She is the author
of four novels and in 1992, she wrote, with Peter
Stanford, Catholics and Sex, *and co-presented the*
Channel 4 documentary series based on the book. As a
journalist, she has worked for Cosmopolitan *and*
She, *and the* Sunday Times. *She is now literary*
editor of the Sunday Express. *On March 6, 1993,*
she became the proud mother of Felix Wells.

Felix and I are watching a video of Walt Disney's *Pinocchio*.
Felix is eating his nightly ration of jelly babies, and I am crying. As the mother of a person just turned three, I am intimate
with the Disney canon, and it invariably reduces me to tears.
It is suitable for small children because they are in their prelap-
sarian state, before the onset of sensitivity that relates to other
people. They can chew and fidget happily, while the griefs
and passions troop past them in searing primaries – the seven
dwarfs sobbing around Snow White's coffin; Simba's

metamorphosis into a cartoon Prince Hamlet when his uncle kills his father; the agony of Dumbo's mother, in chains and screaming for her child.

None of this is suitable for adults. Watching the adventures of the wooden puppet with a soul, I wonder: if that fairy meant to be so kind to Gepetto, why did she grant his wish? The poor old man idly wishes his puppet could be 'a real boy'. Within twenty-four hours, that blameless toymaker is a basket-case, toiling through the streets in pouring rain, searching for his lost baby. Far too quickly, Gepetto has learnt that parental joy is always mixed with pain.

I sympathise, because I made the same wish. Every time I knelt at the altar-rail in church, I would watch the priest blessing the heads of the babies, and pray for a child of my own. My prayer was heard, and I was admitted to the most intense joy on this earth. But I was not prepared for the sorrow of it all.

I have shed tears over my real boy, every single day of his life. Before I had him, I liked to think of myself as a temperate and well-ordered sort of person. Actually, I turn out to be a demented maenad, who screams and hurls plates. I am a soggy, boggy Niobe; a battered victim utterly beset and cowed by testosterone. Our relationship neatly encapsulates the ancient and world-wide power-struggle between men and women.

I love Felix to distraction. I am sure the love would be exactly the same temperature if I had been blessed with a daughter instead, but doubt that I would be enslaved in quite the same way. It is the stormiest love affair of my life. If this was a real love affair, my friends would beg me to leave him.

He beats me like a gong, then melts me with his remorse afterwards.

Those baby hands strike out the chords with unerring skill. He plays me with fascination, checking my reactions minutely. When his true, reciprocal passion for me slips out, it means his guard is down. He has to make up for it with a show of brutality later.

I can follow the processes of Felix's mind, because he talks with extraordinary fluency, but is not yet old enough to hide the machinery.

'If I cry and scream when you go out,' he says, 'Daddy will have to show me his computer, to cheer me up.'

'Yes,' he says comfortably, when kissed by his parents. 'I'm extremely precious, aren't I?'

Appropriately, when he was very tiny, he liked to startle people by suddenly shouting; 'Sigmund Freud!'

Imagine Dr Johnson, sitting on a car seat and wearing a little red hat like a condom. In a deep, measured voice, he tells us a story. 'Once upon a time, I was lying in my bed with the window open, and some bees flew in. And some ladybirds, and some butterflies. And some bugs. And while I was asleep, they peed and poohed all over me. And Daddy came in, when it was morning, and said, "Good grief!" And I had to have a bath.'

. I think this is rather meaningful. So much in life consists of scraping off heaps of butterfly-shit – invisible to the naked eye, but you know it is there.

To glimpse the workings of his mind is, usually, a delight. I once caught him pulling at his toes, immensely serious. 'No,' he murmured to himself, 'they won't come off.' Decisively, he added, 'Because I am *not* a Pobble.'

Occasionally, he is uplifting. 'Let's light a candle, Mummy, and make Our Lady happy.' I, who pride myself upon the rational way in which I communicate my religion, catch myself thinking I have given birth to a saint. Sometimes, he is downright disturbing: 'I used to do that when I was big, before I was born.' Increasingly, however, his verbal gifts are hammered into swords.

'I need sweets and a present to make me happy, because I'm *so* sad.'

'Why are you sad, darling? Did you have a bad dream?'

'Yes. Yes I did.' Visibly, he seizes upon this, and turns it over. 'I dreamt a robber stole me.' Seeing a look on his mother's face as if he had dragged his nails down a blackboard, he adds, 'I dreamt someone killed me.'

I imagine I go to great lengths to shield him from my worst fears, and all the time I am wearing them on my sleeve.

His own worst fears have a flavour of guilty conscience. 'Mummy, when I get sent to prison, you'll be very lonely without your baby.'

Felix's personification of himself as 'your baby' is a naked ploy to pile on the agony, often used for purposes of manip- ulation. For instance, he once persuaded my brother to take him into the Aladdin's Cave of his office, by plaintively observing, 'Poor Bill is crying for his baby.'

I feel sometimes that all this has got out of hand. That the balance of power between us is not quite as it should be. Wasn't I supposed to be the one in charge? Urgent Memo to Mother-Ship: beaming down my commanding officer in the body of a human three-year-old was a terrible idea. Send reinforcements immediately . . .

In the middle of intense and complicated negotiations with him, a mist lifts from my eyes, and I see how little he is. He really is a baby, for God's sake. I am being ruled by someone with dimpled knuckles.

A baby, but a shockingly self-aware one, constantly revolving the advantages that might or might not accrue to the state of babydom. He is always checking his little cousin, eighteen months younger than himself, for signs of usurpation. He cannot decide whether to compete with her in the baby stakes, or flaunt his superior age and attainments.

'Elsa can't talk, can she?'

'Not as well as you,' says Elsa's mother tactfully, 'but she knows lots of words. She can say "dog", and "cat", and—'

'Can she,' interrupts Felix sternly, 'say "microwave"?'

God, I'm sorry for his wife. And she will probably blame me. I have shown him the power he has over me and – it being the only power he has – he abuses it left and right.

A few nights ago, when I was alone in the house with him, he reduced me to sobs of exhausted despair, because he kept dragging me from my bed with impossible demands for sweets, television and bottles of milk. I am sorry to say that in the end we were in competition, to see who could howl the loudest.

'Stop this game!' he rapped out furiously.

'What bloody game?'

'This crying-thing – stop it at once!'

Believe me, I would gladly stop this crying-thing, if only I could stop taking everything so personally. Pope's Poor Indian found God in clouds, and Felix's poor mother finds unbearable poignancy everywhere. Never mind the evening news, or the novels of Dostoevsky. I get to the last page of Shirley Hughes's *Lucy and Tom's Christmas*, and cannot utter the words, 'Happy Christmas, Lucy and Tom, happy Christmas everyone!' without my voice suddenly shooting up an octave, as if I had swallowed a helium balloon. Tears rush to my eyes whenever Postman Pat performs one of his many acts of kindness. I bleed for Eeyore, on his forgotten birthday.

Having a baby buggers up your emotions. We are all in chains. 'A sword shall pierce your heart,' Simeon told Mary, as she carried the infant Jesus into the Temple. He might have added that a sword shall pierce the heart of every mother in the world.

In a playground we frequent there is a bench dedicated to the memory of a son who died in his early twenties. Felix demands to know what that writing says. As I read him the inscription, I commune in imagination with those poor parents. I wonder if his mother brought him to play here, when he was a little thing like my Felix. And I hug my boy's protesting, chunky body, as if I would never let him go. You get an extra station on the dial when you have given birth, and the airwaves are suddenly full of the sound of Rachel weeping.

Post-natal depression always, always has a cause. This fact is entirely overlooked in all the babycare manuals – indeed, in most writing about depression. We will never be able to do a thing about it, until we admit it is there for a reason.

In my baby books, post-natal depression appeared alongside iron deficiency, piles, mastitis and various other afflictions visited on the new mother – things that pop up, without warning, on the tit or bum, and can be assuaged with pills or creams. One or two of the gurus did mention that 'professional' women in their thirties seemed especially vulnerable. Then again, very young and poor mothers are equally at risk. Single mothers get it, because they are all alone. Married mothers get it, because they are not. What do these women have in common? Despair, I would imagine. Whatever the differences in their outer lives, they are all finding the price of motherhood mighty high.

Let's not go into it too deeply, lest we awaken all kinds of awkward issues, such as class and the lowly social status of mothers; men and their enormous reluctance to assume the mantle of fatherhood; money and the difficulty of earning it while breast-feeding. I am still looking for the exact place to put the pin.

Perhaps I should date my depression from the bodily upheaval of pregnancy. We had trundled along fairly quietly together for thirty-two years, my body and I. Like an unexciting but reliable old car — a Volvo, say — it had given me hardly a lick of trouble in all that time. Its weight neither rose nor fell. Its skin was serviceable and unlined.

And then I got pregnant. I gave up smoking, and became hugely fat. In the final month, I had severe oedema, and had to waddle to the jeweller's, to have my wedding ring sawn off my finger. Looking back, this seems highly symbolic. My body had chosen Felix, and elected to slough off his father. It had become a gro-bag, for the protection and nurturance of someone far more important.

The thing inside was also more important than me. I was no longer the heroine of my own life. Sometimes, I wished I could take out the foetus, and leave it to grow in the airing-cupboard. I ate enormously, but without enjoyment, as if under orders. Seditious elements were working inside me, towards a fascist coup.

This was not a bloodless coup. My Winter Palace was stormed and my Reichstag torched. There was some kind of problem at my local hospital, which meant they were short of beds. I was fifteen and a half stone and two and a half weeks overdue before the bastards got round to inducing me. My feet had swollen out of every pair of shoes I owned. I had no neck to speak of, and could barely buckle my watch around a wrist like a Virginia ham.

Finally, I shuffled into hospital, feeling grotesque and humble, and somehow disgraced. At times like this, you realise how little feminism has done for us, and how many miles it has to travel. Joy and fulfilment – what a load of bollocks. There is nothing more patronised, helpless and despised than a big fat woman about to give birth. The moment I arrived in the maternity ward, I realised I was poised at the edge of a vortex of absolute humiliation.

All around me lay vast, bruised whales, in various stages of parturition. Nobody looked nice, and none of us was happy. We were in prison; frisked at the gates for our pride. Women who had already had their babies regarded them with panic-stricken horror, still reeling from the indignity of labour. If you tried to admire their infants, they met you with a dull stare of mutiny.

The midwives were kind. They were sorry for us, and that was awful, because it was an admission that there was nothing they could do. The doctors were as considerate as anyone

can be who spends fourteen hours a day eyeballing a lot of
swollen fannies.

I spent that first night reading *The Pickwick Papers* (my stan-
dard comfort-book, more soothing than the Bible) and
weeping in the lavatory. This was a hideous place, full of vast
bins for bloody dressings the size of paving stones. It ponged
of smoke, because there was an unbearable slag on the ward
who had not given up fags for the duration. She had not had
my advantages, and I ought to have been sorry for her. In fact,
I hated her. I hated everyone. It was like being a new girl at a
really dreadful boarding-school.

If I pressed my nose against the window, I could see cars
streaming down the hill outside. In the city around me, people were going to theatres or restaurants, or just home. Never
had normal life looked so inviting, so glamorous. Several
times, I thought of ringing my husband, demanding to be
taken away. But away where? At this stage, there would be no
escape. Felix was an accomplished fact.

Three long days later, they eventually hauled him out of
me, with dynamite and a pneumatic drill. They thought they
had better give me a Caesarian, when I started on my third
shift of midwives. I had been lying, immobile from the
epidural, in the same room for more than eighteen hours.
Fortunately, I had had pethidine on top of the epidural. The
drugs were good, I will say that. Pethidine does nothing for
the pain, but it pushes time into fast-forward.

It also makes you behave as if at a cocktail party. I laugh and
blush to picture myself now, beached on one of those delivery
beds, legs splayed, fanny split and grinning, conversing with
the midwives like the Queen on an official visit. 'Where do

you take your break, Doreen? And which part of Ireland do you hail from, exactly?'

They must have seen it all, of course. A friend's husband distinguished himself in the delivery room by taking away her TENS machine and strapping it to his bad back. Another friend of mine, convinced she would bellow obscenities in labour, amazed herself by blurting out 'Gosh!' and 'Crikey!' We were all luckier than another friend, who farted throughout like a coalman's drayhorse. No matter how your labour progresses, it is ten to one you will end up making a dick of yourself. Now, there's a fact I don't recall seeing in Miriam Stoppard.

The operation was the best bit of giving birth. After eighteen hours of staring at the same patch of hospital car-park, knowing you will have a baby in ten minutes makes for variety, and perks up the spirits no end. They wheeled me into theatre, gave me more drugs, and sawed me in half like a conjuror's assistant. They also half-shaved my pubes into a goatee. I did not realise this until a few weeks later, when I saw my naked self in a mirror, looking as if I had Catweazle wedged between my legs. Oh, well. I had a sadder beard than anything you could find on a jazz musician, but at least it wasn't on my face.

Reader, have you ever had a Caesarian section? What a curious experience it is. You feel them rummaging about in your vitals. Suddenly, you know what it is to be a sock-drawer.

'This is a big one,' remarked the surgeon, slicing away. 'Any bets on the weight?'

A squelching sound, as of a gumboot being dragged from a bog. Then, from behind the green sheet they put up to shield parents from what must be a revolting sight, a peevish snuffle. Amazingly, there was a baby in the room. My baby. I wanted to reach out for him, but could not move. Tears trickled down into my ears. If I slip back into that moment at the hour of my death, and hear that sound again, I will know there is a God.

The surgeon held my boy above the sheet. I close my eyes, and I can see him now. His sparse dark hair was plastered to his skull, in African curls. One open eye made a blurry but essentially disapproving circuit of the room. He was magnificent. He weighed a whisker under ten pounds. Under the circumstances, I felt the doctor had a cheek, telling me I had put on too much weight. Did he think I hadn't noticed?

Being stitched hurt like hell. Between roars, however, I kept craning around, to see Felix's fat, jowly face in the crook of his father's arm. For months, I had known I was expecting a boy. I had been carrying round the muddy photos of my scan, apparently taken from the Hubble Telescope and purporting to show a tiny penis and scrotum. But nothing had prepared me for the shock of that first meeting. How often, after all, do you meet someone for the first time, already knowing you will love them passionately?

Who was he? Would I like him? Would he like me? I thought him very lovely, with his Martian helmet of a head and his honks of bad temper. But I could not shake off the eerie feeling that he disapproved of me – are you her, are you all?

I disapproved of myself. I was suddenly face to face with my deep, deep inadequacy. I look back at the very beginning of his life, and I am filled with shame. I was everything this poor little creature had in the world, and all I wanted to do was sleep. I was obsessed with sleep. The peace of it. The privacy of it. Sometimes, late at night, I fantasised about us both being dead, and lying together in our coffin.

He gnawed at my sore breasts, and my tears fell – splat, splat, splat – upon his innocent head. Here was the crying-thing, in its dreary dawn. Also the fearful thing, the hopeless thing, the despairing thing. I clung to Felix all the more desperately, because I thought I could see everything else I had vanishing down the plughole.

I think I did lose a great deal. I am not the woman I was, before I got pregnant. The woman I have become is thin and rather anxious, with bags under her eyes and lines on her face. There is nothing wrong with her, but she is a stranger. I haunt mirrors, as I did when adolescent, to check that nothing else has cropped up or dropped off. Even three years on, it is hard not to feel as if I were recovering from a car crash. My whole life was smashed and splintered, and I am still crunching the shards underfoot.

Sleep is no longer an obsession, however, nor even a necessity. It has become a hobby. At last, I have the key to the phenomenon of Margaret Thatcher. She is the mother of twins. She discovered she could get by on four hours' sleep a night, and the nation never looked back. I do rather admire her, when I remember how peculiar I was, on four hours' sleep. I am not prime minister material, evidently.

Mrs Thatcher and I, however, share something that – in my opinion – renders us both unsuitable for high office. We are the mothers of sons. Anyone who doubts the effects of having a male child on the mother's lobes has only to look at Mrs T.

Her one vulnerable place is her boy. When the idiotic Mark got lost in the desert, we were all treated to the sight of our First Citizen as a weeping old Mum. A female PM with a son, I suspect, is as much a political liability as a male PM who owns a gay brothel.

If her daughter had been the wanderer, Mrs T would have been brisk and confident – girls can look after themselves. Boys can't. I swore I would never be like this, if I had a son, but it must be in the hormones – mothers vigorously build their sons up, but secretly treat them as stretcher-cases, who need to be nursed through every minute of the day. Suppose Felix were at a boarding-school (which heaven forbid now, but ask me again in twelve years), I would be the kind of mother who is always ringing the house-master, nagging him about my darling's warm pants. Where Felix is concerned, I will always be Kanga, in *Winnie The Pooh*, only ever seen counting little Roo's vests.

If he had been a girl, I would probably worry less. I'd assume a daughter would be as tough and reliable as I am. I have realised, as the mother of a son, that the entire male sex would collapse without the army of women supporting it. My job turns out to be making a man of my boy. And I am not talking about stiffening his upper lip. or ordering him never to cry. A man's mother is less than perfect if she does not devote herself to telling him he is utterly wonderful and vastly superior to the rest of the world. She has to believe it, too.

The rewards are enormous. All mothers of sons drivel on about how gorgeous, how melting it is, when the little fellow lisps: 'I love you, Mummy.' I usually have to wait until Felix is about to topple into sleep, or bolting a chocolate. But I know he loves me, and that sends me into a frenzy of protectiveness. I long to live up to the standards he has set for me.

He has strong notions of what is suitable. 'Take all that stuff off your face!' he thunders, seeing me dressed for the outside world. 'Get that paint off your nails!'

Felix likes a pretty girl. He is very interested in the rows of Barbie dolls at Woolworth's. 'I am a boy,' he says, 'but I am a boy who likes Barbies.' Basically, he fancies them, but this does not mean he wants to see his own womenfolk flaunting themselves in bikinis. I tried to give him a non-sexist upbringing, and got Mr Machismo anyway.

'I'm just *mending* a few things with my *drill*, Mum. You go in the kitchen and make my dinner.'

Yes, dear. Have I to call you, or shall I leave it in a saucer on t'range?

The courtiers of Louis XIV vied for the honour of watching him have a crap. Felix I likes me to sit meekly outside the lavatory, making light conversation, while he voids his bowels with the door open. Visitors to the house are often invited to share the spectacle. 'I'm just popping upstairs to do a pooh. You can come too, if you like.'

It is an honour for me to watch. With Felix's father, the roles are reversed and the honour lies in being watched. Felix idolises his father.

'Daddy,' he sighs, 'has such a lovely big willy. Where's your willy, Mummy?'

'I'm a woman. Women don't have them.'

'Did Daddy take yours away?'

Daddy takes things away when they are dangerous, or being naughtily misused.

Sigmund Freud! Dr Freud to Reception, please.

Once again, I am sorry for his wife. I now know why love affairs are shaped as they are, and why the words 'fairness' and 'romance' are so seldom found in the same sentence. I am the breadwinner in our house, but Felix sees emotional rather than economic power. A father's attention must be striven for and won. A mother's is a given. Her body has no boundaries, her time has no limits. I have had the greatest difficulty explaining to my little son why I have to work.

'Because I have to make money, for us all to live on. If I didn't work, we wouldn't be able to buy any food.'

Felix protests, 'But I'm not hungry!'

And notwithstanding the fact I have to work all the hours God sends to keep us solvent, I feel wicked. I am sure I shall sink into his consciousness as a selfish, rejecting harpy. I can hear him in thirty years' time, telling his analyst he can't form relationships with women, because his mother kept going upstairs to work when he was a baby. She paid another woman to take care of him – thus carving into his mind the message that taking care of children is always women's work.

He may also get the message that it is menial work. I cannot deny that comes from me. No matter how adored and wonderful the child, child-care is boring drudgery; especially if you have got used to having a proper life. I do find the restriction of it, and the Lilliputian level, very wearing.

Once upon a time, when I was still childless, I met a friend of mine wheeling her baby along the High Street.

I asked, 'How are you?'

With a glassy smile, she trilled, 'We haven't decided whether to go the swimming-pool or the toy library – have

we, sweetie?' (This last addressed to the surly Mussolini type
in the buggy.)

Nanny-work, I thought. And still think. Even if I did not
have to work, I would probably want to. I can't do those
Mummyish things for more than twenty minutes at a stretch,
without sneaking out for a smoke and a strong coffee. Please
do not assume, however, that I am at all squeamish about the
mess.

I can wipe noses and bums with the best of them. In fact,
I am thinking of using my garnered wisdom to write a
learned monograph about baby-shit. How it is dark green
gloop called 'meconium' when they are first born, and you
need a blowtorch to get it off their cheeks. How parents may
expect, in the earliest months, a phenomenon we professionals call 'a yellow-leg job' – a canary-coloured excretion that
has dyed the entire leg of a Babygro. How a small baby can,
without apparently moving, squirt the stuff right up its back.
How small-talk about ordure will always get you through any
sticky social situation with a three-year-old.

But I digress. It is only too easy, with such a packed Variety bill as my Felix. Following in lightning succession, we
have slapstick, comedy and pathos. With his lashes still wet
from the last tantrum, he launches into a song, and shouts:
'Did you like that, ladies and gentlemen? Let's have it *again*!'

That is something else I will hear when I die, if heaven
exists. It is droll to hear Felix singing along with his George
Formby tape: 'I go cleaning *winders*, to earn an honest *bob*,/
For a nosey parker, it's an interesting *job*!' So why am I crying
again?

Over his gusto, I suppose, and the completeness of his

pleasure. When he is that happy, I am already looking ahead to the moment when the happiness turns to grief. I want to be ready to catch him, and know there will always be falls I cannot break.

Sometimes, I long for him to grow up. Mostly, I dread it. At every stage, I have wanted him to stay just at that point, but there is something especially enchanting about a three-year-old. Perhaps that is what that poor, bereaved mother thought, when she put the memorial to her son on the bench in the playground. In some parallel universe, where Time is not, there will always be a place for me, where my beautiful three-year-old Felix is playing.

M y M u m

PHINEAS FOSTER

Phineas Foster was born in December 1981. Apart from one year with his family in Princeton, New Jersey, and a spell in Dublin, he has lived in London all his life. He has a ten-year-old sister, Nora, and attends University College School. Phineas has reviewed teenage fiction for the Independent on Sunday.

Staring at her makes you laugh
(I don't know why!)
Our eyes are locked together
Like heat-seeking missiles and an enemy plane
Her hair is black like the deep dark night
Her ears are quite small like tiny little shells
Her personality changes at every time of the day
She scratches my back
(Where I can't reach)
She cares for me like a leopard and her cub
She's my mother and I love her.

I wrote that poem when I was nine. I'm fourteen now, and in

the time that has passed I have slowly started to see my mother in a different light. As I get older she seems to get younger. We are beginning to watch and listen to the same things. I always thought she was a fountain of knowledge, perfect in every way. I suppose I saw her in the same way as any young child views his mother, but it is only now that I can look back and see how little of my mother I actually knew.

My mother was born in Dublin, where she attended day school and university. She came to London in her early twenties after she had married my Dad. They waited nine years to have children. They say I was planned.

My mother can still make me laugh. Her readiness for a dirty joke often shocks my father, and after only five minutes of her company you forget that she is your mother. Sometimes I find myself telling her things that no boy would tell either of his parents. That can be both embarrassing and dangerous. She seems to enjoy the company of children more than that of some adults. She likes to be around young people – I think it makes her feel young herself. She's a very forward character. Whereas most mothers step aside and let their children entertain their own friends, my mother, more often than not, wants to join in. When they're in the room she can have a complete mood-swing, from forty-five-year-old cynic to cheeky fourteen-year-old, up for anything. I don't know which is worse. It must feel quite strange to those who visit. Local friends have grown accustomed to her jibes and upfront attacks; they give as good as they get, and sometimes even better.

Her friends and I have always got on. She has a very particular taste when it comes to who she keeps company with, my Dad being the exception. She will never settle for economists or bankers, preferring the artistic type. Without meaning to sound like a lonely hearts letter in *Time Out*, she likes people who can hold her attention for more than five minutes. This is not easy. She likes a good row, too. When I was younger and she got tired of screaming at me she used to throw me out of the house. I'm bigger than she is now, so she can't do that any more. I got tired of ringing the neighbour's doorbell with some excuse about a lost ball, so I could climb over the wall into our back garden. Last summer in Kerry she had the row of the century. A friend of hers from Dublin – a very noisy barrister at the best of times – said something over dinner about forgiving German war crimes, and my Mum was on to him like a wildcat. I could still hear them fighting as I went to sleep, and woke up at three as they roared at each other out on the landing. They were still at it over breakfast; I felt quite sorry for her friend by the time they decided to bury the hatchet some time that evening.

These days most of our rows are about schoolwork. If I underachieve I am jumped on. She is permanently suspicious of my motives when I go to my room to work. Perhaps it's because, like me, her biggest problem is organisation, so whenever she lectures me about filing and neatness I can only whisper, 'Hypocrite.' I suppose she recognises herself in me. We can both do the work we're set, in fact, we're both quite good at it, but somehow things are last-minute and done in a panic – totally different to Dad and my sister. But because she knows me so well, she believes in me completely. For that reason my parents probably hold the trophy for Most Troublesome Parents of All Time. They hate it when a teacher tells them I'm no good at something – they think it's my laziness or his bad teaching, and they say so.

I've had to train my Mum to keep her mouth shut at football matches. When I was younger she used to take me to White Hart Lane (she had to take me because the first match my Dad ever got tickets for he was so bored with the idea he tried to bring a book). My Mum quite likes football, and at first she thought being a Spurs supporter was about learning to be 'a good sport' and praising the other team. When she clapped Forest's first goal I nearly died. Judging by the dirty looks she got from all around the stand she was lucky to escape with her life. She's harder to control when she comes to watch me play. I always beg her to come, which is stupid. Every time she's there I get injured. The last time I tore a hamstring. As I lay writhing in pain on the pitch I could hear her laughing with the other mothers, saying what a faker I had always been. Screams from the touchline such as 'Give it more welly!' make me want to kick her, but she just thinks it's funny.

Only one time I've seen her go really quiet. A bomb scare had us banging about outside the Tottenham ground before a big game. The police were pushing and shoving us and the fans were getting really angry, screaming abuse at them and swearing among themselves about the 'f***ing Irish'. Usually, in circumstances like that, you can expect my mother to make a scene: this is a woman who has thrown Rottweiler owners out of dog-free zones and embarrassed me in restaurants, cinemas and bus queues since before I could speak. But this time she kept quiet, making us walk right away from the action and wait for hours down a boring side street. Until that day I had never noticed her Dublin accent.

Every summer we spend about a month in County Kerry, in the house which belonged to her grandfather and is now my great-aunt's. She's been going there since she was a baby and I know she loves it more than anywhere in the world. This may be because it's where her own mother grew up, and even though she died nine years ago she still feels very close to her. It's funny for me to meet people who remember my mother when she was my age, and it's the opposite of impersonal London. Milltown is a very easy place to be, lots of aunts, cousins and everyone knowing your name, wanting to catch up with your news. My Mum has lived in England now for over twenty years, but it is only in Kerry that I think she comes into her own. It's also the only place where she does not seem so different to other mothers.

As I grow older, music is one subject about which we seem to agree more and more. My first real mother–son bonding session was a Guns 'n' Roses concert in the Milton Keynes Superbowl. I was eleven (so I don't want this held against me) and G 'n' R were the first band that I ever really cared about. I had missed them at Wembley the summer before, so it seemed to me to be my mother's duty to get tickets that April and drive me up the M1. All along the motorway she lectured me about the dangers of rock concerts: the drugs, violence, drunks, and going to the toilet alone. She claimed that when it came to rock festivals she was a veteran. By the time we arrived she had me shitting myself.

The Superbowl didn't seem so super when we got there. It was three-thirty in the afternoon and our group weren't expected until nine; the weather was arctic, the rain was pissing down steadily, there was nowhere to sit except on muddy grass slopes and concrete runways; furthermore there were no interesting junkies or drunks or leather-clad bikers – only thousands upon thousands of eleven-year-old kids with their forty-something mothers. By five o'clock we had sampled all the fast food, bought a T-shirt or three and listened to the usual boring support bands.

That was when my Mum spoke to the security guard by the stage. I think he took pity on her. He issued us both with passes to come and go to the car so we could warm up, and then he asked, 'Would you like to stand in here?' He was offering us the chance to stand right under the stage, inside the crash barrier of screaming, fainting fans. It was really brilliant. I could nearly touch Axel Rose (kitted in a Charles Manson T-shirt which my Mum said was really sick), and even though I think they're rubbish now I have to admit they gave a really good concert.

We got home well after midnight and by two in the morning I was vomiting up three donuts, two sticks of candy floss, hundreds of penny sweets, four hamburgers and numerous gallons of soft drink. My mother had forgotten to warn me about the dangers of fast food. Later, I heard her tell how depressed she was at being identified as 'a mother' by the security guard: safe enough to be let near the stage, with no danger of her leaping on to the stage and tearing off Axel Rose's jock-strap.

Since then our musical tastes have got a lot closer. I never really hit it off with all the old sixties stuff until I got into bands like Oasis and Pulp and discovered her record collection. I was the first in the family to own a CD player, but more and more I think some of the best sounds seem to be on vinyl. When Mum and Dad finally forked out the money for a modern sound system, I was gifted the record player plus loads of their discarded LPs. Now I sit upstairs listening to the Beatles and the Kinks while they sit downstairs listening to my CDs.

My parents have always tried to convince me how poor we are. Things have got worse since my parents gave up on the state school system and told me they were 'investing' in my future. They moan a lot about money, and my mother, who is a freelance writer, seems to be permanently broke. Despite this, she is a shopping addict. In the years before I could cling to the doorway of Fenwick's and refuse to enter, she dragged me from sweaters to bras and back again. When she saw an item of clothing, usually in black or red, she'd go for it, reduced or not. I noticed that when she *did* find something cheap on sale she never saw it as a saving: it was an excuse to buy more.

Now I realise that I am no better. I blame her genes. Occasionally, my father attempts to drum this fault out of us. He doesn't stand a chance. In fact, when we go shopping together these days, the results can be stratospheric. I usually buy my casual wear with my own money, but if we see something really ace, she may buy it for me. If the thing comes in black or red, she may even buy me two. Now that I think about it, we dress in the same sort of style. Not dresses and tights, but we wear the same colours and seem to put separates together in the same sort of way. Like her, I often sneak in with something smart from Camden Lock and keep the price-tag well concealed from my father. One day, shopping will be the end of us.

An expense my mother complains about a lot these days is her car insurance. I was nine when she lost her licence for drink-driving. A small problem with a one-way street and a panda car, her failure to blow into the breathalyser (she had bronchitis, or so she says) and automatic arrest. A blood test revealed that she was just three points over the limit. She still claims the magistrates apologised when they banned her for a year, and it makes a good story when she tells it, but it was a hellish year. My Dad is away in Oxford for most of the week, which meant the ordinary trips like school runs, football matches, visits to friends and days out suddenly got very complicated. The only advantage to all that time spent in other people's cars or waiting for public transport was a great sense of pride; it was a real buzz telling other parents about my law-bending mother. Some of them could look really shocked, and none of my friends had a Mum like that.

As the year went by I couldn't help noticing how much my mother was changing. She had always been a good driver. In fact, it was her job to take the wheel on the gruelling journeys to and from Ireland. Left at home or in the passenger seat she seemed different, quieter, almost depressed. She was lousy at navigating (previously Dad's forte), and long drives seemed to be longer and became more tense than ever. Things are normal again now, with my mother back in the driving seat. She looks right there.

I think my mother has mellowed over the years. We seem to fight less than we used to. She just says she's got older and weaker. She has definitely got smaller. From the eight-foot giant of my infancy she has shrunk to a mere five foot two and can't reach my back to scratch it without a stepladder. Old photographs from the '60's and '70's show a younger, thinner version with long, naturally coloured hair and hippy-looking clothes. She's always on holidays, tanned and happy, with no babies in sight. Nowadays, her hair isn't quite as midnightish either, more a bleak grey winter evening despite all those hours locked in the bathroom with Capital Radio and a box of Recital hair dye. But people tell me she's still good-looking.

I don't know how my mother will react to this piece. She may very well sulk, or laugh, and there's a slight possibility of anger. She will certainly be very critical of my writing skills. But knowing her, these negative feelings will only last a day or two, so I'm keeping my head down and my fingers crossed. It has been an interesting exercise. I have never thought about her in such depth before. She has always just been my Mum. But having written all this, I've come out of it knowing a lot more about her, and our relationship. Like the leopard and her cub in my poem, I realise that she is still there for me, still screaming encouragement from the sidelines, still embarrassing me like hell.

The Prince of Castle Air

SUSAN RICHARDS

Susan Richards' first book, Epics of Everyday Life, *was about Russia under glasnost. Her second, to be published soon, is about post-Soviet Russia. She produced nine films with David Puttnam and now runs a company with her husband, writer and filmmaker Roger Graef.*

(Biographical note: Max was born in 1979. His parents, both Americans living in London, split up in 1983. A year later his father and I got together. We were married in 1986. It was my first marriage and I had no children. Later that year Max's mother was killed in a car accident in Portugal, where she had been living with Max and his sister.)

'Happy families are all alike', pronounced Tolstoy: 'every unhappy family is unhappy in its own way.' Once, I might have been seduced by the confidence of such an assertion, but not now. The old man, an insufferable husband himself, was just wrong.

Tolstoy certainly wrote better about unhappy families than he did about happy ones and I can understand why. Happiness is harder to put into words: its language is mimsy and uffish. Emotional clichés block the way like burnt-out cars.

When the subject is not some fictional family but my own, language is only the first of the obstacles. There is also hubris: if I expose my happiness to the light, will it turn to dust? Worse still, will I find that I am living in a fantasy?

I would love to be confident that Max, the boy whom, with inflamed pride, I call my son, is happy. But they do inhabit another country, the young, and when they speak our language they do so out of kindness, translating, censoring what we would not understand. I read Max's poems and I am frightened by the darkness of the images in which he clothes his feelings.

So I will be careful not to attribute happiness to him. But this I know: wherever he goes he brings it with him. Today he left the house in the middle of the night by his clock (8.00 a.m. adult time) to start his first steady holiday job. Within a week the reports will be trickling back. How we love to have Max around, they will say, such a gentle presence, so cheerful, conscientious, considerate.

I know too that everything he undertakes with his heart turns to quality; that when he plays roller hockey in Hyde Park his figure against the Albert Memorial has a dancer's grace; that when he writes about Dickens in a school essay the impact of his words sends me spinning back to the book about which he writes; that as a friend and a son he is true. I cannot presume to say that Max is happy but I know that a boy who was once broken has become whole.

There is a particular reason why, for all my dizzy pride in my son, I tiptoe around the issue of family happiness. With us it did not descend like a fairy's kiss. By painful degrees it was constructed out of the wreckage of a random event that killed Max's mother.

After the accident I knew what I was in for: duty, not happiness. I had been dealt a role that was beyond my character and range. However hard I tried, I would be cast for life as the Wicked Stepmother. Had I thought about change at all at that stage, I might have said that if I stuck at it I had the power to change Max's life for the better. But the idea that he might transform mine – that never crossed my mind.

No one could have told me that I might get a son who considered it his filial duty to make me have fun. Giving would be a one-way business, I assumed. Gratitude was not something which I ever expected to feel or to get. Yet Max never punished me for not being his mother. From early on he expressed his gratitude to me generously and with dignity:

9th March 1991

Dear Susie,

I am the Prince of Castle Air, a place not known by thee. Thou art a loving person to I, and I'm always pleased to be with thee. Thou has tried so hard for me, and thou art appreciated for thy niceness to me. Thou art a person to turn to for me, helping me and caring for me, acting as if thou were my mother.

I am very grateful and hope that I am not in any way a hindrance to thou.

Yours happily, gratefully and hopefully

The Castle Air Prince of
XAM   (put near a mirror)

Thanks to the Prince of Castle Air, as he called himself in this letter written when he was eleven, I write now in defence of the 'broken' family. Stories like *Cinderella* and *Hamlet* tell us that the bond between the parent and the child is irreplaceable, and those who step into a parent's shoes poison everything they touch. But in our culture, in which one out of every three marriages fails, huge numbers of us live with parents and children who are not our own.

The broken family is a unit that asks too much of each of us. But in doing so it offers us the chance of changing in ways we would never have done if our lives had gone as they 'ought' to have done. I have a sense that, because of the effort we have made, Max and I have behaved better to each other than we would probably have done to our biological mother or son.

While we may hang on to the idea of a 'real' family as a paradise lost, with the other half of our brains we know that life with Cinderella's absentee father or Hamlet's silly mother would have had its problems.

I did not need to know what it was that had destroyed the marriage of Max and Chloe's American parents, for all their hard work. Those problems were written all over the children when their father first introduced us. Chloe was eleven and Max was five. We met at the zoo in Regent's Park, but it was cold and grey, so we went to a movie in Leicester Square instead.

They were a strikingly different pair. Everyone liked

Chloe, said she was marvellous. But the strain of being marvellous showed. In *A Night at the Opera*, a film which Max
and I both loved, there is a moment when Groucho Marx,
dressed in his long coat, hides behind a cabin door by hook-
ing himself up on a coat-hanger. Chloe's shoulders looked
like Groucho on a coat-hanger; she had dark pits under her
eyes that never seemed to go away. She was afraid of her
father, and afraid for her mother. She carried on those shoulders the weight of their failed marriage, of her mother's
confidences. She looked like a child, but there was no room
for childhood in her life.

Max, well, Max looked like an angel: blond curls, cherubic
lips, snub nose. He still had chubby baby limbs and his skin
felt like rose petals. But he came with a reputation. People
talked about him as if he were a little monster: tyrannical, full
of tantrums and sulks. I was surprised, that first day, how
much I enjoyed his company.

I went on enjoying it. Yes, Max could be moody if he did
not get his own way. But in retrospect it is clear that the two
children simply reacted in opposite ways to the troubles that
were raining down on them. While Max acted out his griefs,
his sister, in the way of women, hoped to make it all right for
everyone by holding hers in.

In those first two years I had only a bit-part in Max's life.
He and Chloe lived with their mother in the country and
came to us at weekends. His father dealt with his moods, not
me. But moods apart, he was fun. Lacking any role in his life,
I played with him. We wrestled a lot. He loved simple things
like throwing me around. I was a film producer and I was
absorbed by movie-making. But when he threw me around I

had to stop worrying about contracts and neurotic directors. He taught me how to play again.

For Max and Chloe the big event of that period was their mother's move to Portugal. It must have been paradise for him: sunshine, beaches and, most important of all, the company of boys of his age. He was always gregarious and when his mother and her friend Carol took a house together he acquired, all at once, two brothers in Robbie and Kelly.

For me, marriage to Max and Chloe's father was the big event. I was in my mid-thirties and I had never been married before. 'They', that ominous chorus, had warned me against Max's father as they did against Max. He was charming, they said, but tricky. I took no notice. The wedding was my idea; because of his experience of marriage, Roger was not keen at first. But we both wanted to have more children and I would not start a family unless we were married. Was that just old-fashioned? Maybe, but thank goodness for it, in view of what was about to happen.

I had forgotten, until my father reminded me, how nervous Roger was about broaching the subject of the wedding with Chloe. Being so much her mother's protector, how would she react? Would she even want to come? He underestimated Chloe. She was thirteen only in the most literal sense. 'Come off it, Dad. Of course I'm coming. I want to be a bridesmaid. You know very well how our family's changed since you met Susan. I always used to be afraid of you.' Life was bound to be painful for any child who saw things so clearly.

What can that little American boy have made of such an English occasion? It cannot have been as complicated for him as it was for Chloe. He was still only seven. It was the last great family event at my parents' house, that perfect eighteenth-century dolls' house, set in cedar trees.

The morning was overcast, but our wise friend Alice sent prayers to St Exupéré, the patron saint of lost things and weather and, just in time, the sun burst out and shone on us. Max wore a grey bow-tie, made out of the same silk as his father's cravat. There was dancing in the marquee on the lawn; Uncle John and my cousin Julian sang in the church. Who would have guessed that Max would end up at the ancient public school where my cousin taught music?

The next bit is hard to write about. I am reminded of the White King's problems when he tries to describe to his wife what it was like when a huge, invisible Alice picked him up: 'I assure you, my dear, I turned cold to the very ends of my whiskers!' To which the Queen replies, 'You haven't got any whiskers.' 'The horror of that moment,' the King goes on. 'I shall never, NEVER forget!' 'You will, though,' the Queen says 'if you don't make a memorandum of it.' The White King takes a pencil, but Alice takes control of it from above and writes 'The White Knight is sliding down the poker. He balances very badly.' The Queen comments: 'That's not a memorandum of YOUR feelings!'

Four months after the wedding came the car crash in Portugal which killed the children's mother. I cannot write about that, because it was not my tragedy. But the White Queen was right: you do forget the horror of it. I find that I have covered up the memory with a version that fits in with the way it has turned out, a sweet Happy Families version.

Of Max's feelings there is no memorandum. I can only say what happened. On top of the catastrophe of his mother's death, aged seven he had to leave his home, all his friends, his sister, school, sunshine, everything, and come to London. He had no friends here and he came to an adult household where nothing was geared to children. Even his room at the top of the house was his in name only. The walls were lined with his father's papers and filing cabinets.

Chloe, who was six years older, asked to stay on at school in Portugal. She was too old to coerce, and too wise. We had to let her stay. But Max had no option. Instead of his mother he got me. All this he felt, quite rightly, was a gross injustice.

I felt the same. I had strengths and potential strengths, but being a full-time stepmother was not one of them. I was in the throes of trying to have a child of my own. His mother's death aborted that child. Now that I was married, children had arrived but they were not my children. How dared his mother go and die? It was not romantic to have to recognise that, had the tragedy happened a couple of years earlier, I would probably have been too wary ever to have allowed myself to get close to his father.

I panicked. Using the most professional of reasons I went off to the States, as I had always planned to, for the shooting of a film. It was an excuse. My presence wasn't needed. But in the looking-glass world that Max and I had entered, I clearly needed to set off in the opposite direction in order to get back to Max at all. By the time I arrived home, at least I had had enough of being a producer to last me for a while.

There are many pretty things I could write about that period. But the nearest I can get to the truth is that it probably worked out between Max and me because we were both ill-suited to the roles that had been assigned to us. If I had been the motherly type, Max would doubtless have given me as hard a time as (they said) he had given his mother. But he must have realised early on that that was not going to work on me: if he gave me a hard time, he would get one back.

As for me, had I had that 'real' son instead of Max I would probably have followed the Duchess's recipe for motherhood:

> Speak roughly to your little boy,
> And beat him when he sneezes . . .

But with Max I was constrained by being a Wicked Stepmother. There were so many instincts that I could not give in to. It was even hard to shut the door on him because it felt as if I were shutting him out in a different way than if he had been my 'real' son.

The joke is that I always used to pride myself on never having vented my true feelings on Max. Yes, until now when I look back, I believed that I had spared him. But I must have made him feel in the way. Why otherwise would he have developed the habit, a few years later, of saying 'I'm sorry' all the time?

'Don't keep on saying "sorry",' I'd say.

'Sorry,' he'd reply.

Max remained grateful, I suspect, for the most generous of reasons: not because I succeeded, but because I tried.

To start with I got through my days by making an effort. We made an unspoken contract: I undertook to do my very best for him so long as he was nice to me. I responded to his distress, but not to his sulks. The distress was awful. I had only just arrived back from the filming when the cosy school he was attending sent a letter out to all parents to let us know that the key to the playground had disappeared, immobilising the school's activities. Could we please check to make sure that our child had not taken it? I looked in Max's blue satchel. There it was.

Then, at almost the same time, the money in the petty cash box in our study disappeared. I found it, unspent and almost visible, in a heap on the floor of the linen cupboard. There were so many places in his room where he could have hidden it. But he was not trying to hide it, he was making sure that it would be discovered. He could not have found any way of saying more clearly to his father and me that we had to forget about our problems and pay attention to him, as his need was far greater than ours.

He was indeed the Prince of Castle Air, a place not known by me. When I took him upstairs and showed him what I had found he burst into tears and so did I.

I felt helpless to relieve his distress. His pain was palpable, always there, in the same house as me, my house. He had become a different child. Where he had been fearless and outgoing he was now frail. Conflicting emotions played on his pale face like squalls on a lake. When I put him to bed he would lie awake for hours every night, unable to sleep. His loneliness was terrible. He became a single child, but without the resources that a single child develops. He hated to be on his own. But I could not take him in my arms and comfort him as I would have done before his mother's death. That would have been to trespass on the place she had left behind.

If I wanted to distract or comfort him I had to fight with him. There was never a time when Max was too low for a wrestle or a tickle. It was more than a child's playfulness. While we were fighting he seemed to forget his pain. But it was hard, because whenever I tried to stop he became desperate. I could see the pain flooding back.

Poetry was a great escape. The poems had to be funny. We didn't like them deep, or soppy. Rhythm acted on him like a narcotic, blanking out everything disagreeable. I have just turned up a poem he wrote aged eight, about a year after he came to England under the influence of Eliot's 'Skimbleshanks'. It was written in honour of Ratty, Supreme Rodent, his grey and white room mate:

> *Raturday, Raturday,*
> *For him it's always Saturday.*
> *he explores behind the books*
> *And is fussy with the cooks.*
> *He loves his warm potato,*
> *But won't touch a fresh tomato.*
> *He says that rice*
> *is very nice.*
> *Rats like rice*
> *but so do mice.*
>
> *When Raturday's behind the books,*
> *And playing at a game,*
> *They start falling right and left,*
> *And Raturday's to blame.*
> *We try again to put them back,*

> *And they refuse to stay on stack.*
> *Raturday squeezes through his cage,*
> *He reads his books with every page.*
>
> *He is racing round the room*
> *In a special flying zoom*
> *As he jumps to the bears,*
> *In their special private layers.*
> *We can't squeeze our hand through*
> *Before he goes to the loo.*
> *And we can hear him in there squeaking*
> *While we are left outside there peeking!*

Nonsense was the other escape. Max and I became hooked on *Alice in Wonderland*, *Alice through the Looking Glass* and Edward Lear. Life was all a great deal easier to handle, indeed to enjoy, we discovered, as long as it did not make complete sense.

When Alice was left with the Duchess's baby it turned into a piglet in her arms. The next few years brought similar transitions for us. What it was like for Max I cannot say, but for me, left holding the piglet as it were, it turned by imperceptible degrees into a boy, into my son. As that began to happen the clear edges of our deal became blurred and turned into gratitude. In another of his letters, written when he was a little older he speaks about this transition:

> *Suzzzzzzzzzzzzzzzzzzzzzzzzie,*
> *When I came to London almost six years ago, I was very inconsiderate and selfish and I didn't think that anyone else could feel bad as well. And now I thank you for putting up*

with me, because you've also (I hope) – changed me (for the bet-
ter hopefully!) And if it wasn't for you I wouldn't be me. (That
sounds strange, but it is true.) Because you've taught me to
think about what I'm doing, or what I will do or should do.
And I think I'm much better for that. I also have to thank you
for protecting me from Dad when he used to get in those bad
moods. Putting up with me, understanding and trying to help
all at the same time must be tough.

With tonnes of love and thanx from Max.

As the alliance between the two of us strengthened, it began
to affect other members of the family. Most dramatically, of
course, it touched Max's father.

I did try to protect the children from their father's temper.
It was an old anger, handed down from his own father, and it
sat oddly with his warmth and gaiety. I tried to make him
understand that, whatever they had done to deserve it, as
soon as he became angry he also became wrong.

Years before there was the memorable winter day when
Max decided to leave home. He can have been no older than
nine. I never knew what the row between the two of them
was about. It was after supper. I heard raised voices, heard
Max going upstairs to his room. Rather than stumping up, his
footsteps were quiet and I knew something serious had
happened.

After a while I went up and found him with an open suit-
case, packing to leave. We sat on the floor and talked. This
time it was more than a rage. He really was leaving. What
could I do? I felt the justice of his position, as well as its
weakness, thanks to his age. 'I'll come with you,' I said. And

once again he gave me that look, disbelieving, grateful.

The balance of the family shifted that evening. He knew that I meant what I had said and he understood the implications. When he had come to live in our house two years earlier, I had been his father's wife. What I was saying was that if I were forced to choose roles now, I would opt to be his mother. It was simple: he needed me more than his father did.

He and I walked downstairs hand in hand and went, in trepidation, to the study to tell his father that we were going. It ended in tears and hugs, of course. But from then onwards it was Max's father, not Max, who felt on probation. Either he mastered his temper, or, the implicit threat stood, all three of us might make other arrangements, as Chloe had already done. Since his father adored us he took the ultimatum seriously.

It didn't happen all at once. Like the graft between Max and me it was to take time. But now, ten years after his mother's death, Max's father has changed too. The anger has gone. And as it retreated, the heavy atmosphere in our house lifted. The whiff of imminent recrimination vanished.

The irony is that Max's father is now the man whom, I suspect, Max's mother longed for him to be. It was not something that simply happened with age. Its precondition was the terrible chemistry of the changes, one by one, that began to occur as a result of her death.

There were others, no less remarkable. At the funeral I had talked for the first time to Max's aunt, his mother's younger sister. It did not look as if we had much in common. She lived in London, was a secretary. But with the death of her beautiful, talented sister something happened in her that precipitated her into headlong growth. She became the essential other adult in the children's lives, their connection with their mother, their source of fun and comfort. Ten years later, she has also become managing director of one of Britain's fastest-growing companies. Gradually, she and I, unlikely friends at all, became more than that. We became sisters.

While all these changes were happening at home, Max's life at school looked normal enough. He was growing up to be a handsome boy: slim, slightly elfin, with a gust of uncut curls. When he had arrived over here he was still an American. But we put him into English schools. Our criteria were simple. His mother's death was bound to have laid down a fault-line in him. One of these days, we said to ourselves, he was bound to erupt. It was up to us to find schools where he would be safe whenever this happened. The English schools were the safest places we could find.

He appeared to adjust almost without faltering, to become a successful English schoolboy, a regular prizewinner, a gymnast, playing music, making friends. But still we did not believe that our luck could last. We waited for the fault to claim him. Underneath his facility, we could see the struggle. Although he loved the company of other children, he sometimes seemed a little set apart – the American, looking wistfully on at the ease of those born in a culture that was not his.

But though he felt American, his father had left the States long before he was born and his mother's culture was a memory that was growing fainter with every day. It could only be topped up by wearing bright clothes and baseball caps and watching American football on Sunday evenings.

His teachers must have found us tiresome, over-solicitous,

waiting always for that fault-line to open up. Then one day, when he was fifteen, his present house-master turned on us: 'You must stop worrying about Max. If only all my boys had Max's problems. He is stalwart.'

Stalwart. The word pulled us up short. It was a word that belonged to another, more stable time. That it should apply to Max . . . 'Stalwart,' we repeated wonderingly to one another, with tears in our eyes, as if he had just been declared a prodigy. His house-master was right, of course. Drawing back our veil of anxiety we found that the fault-line had disappeared.

I think Max always was stalwart. I remember the first night he slept in London after his mother's death. I put him to bed in the room next door to ours, which we had been using as a dressing room. We had just decorated it with an expensive wallpaper. Against a Chinese-red background, enormous lilies and lily pads wound their way up the room.

Unable to sleep, Max looked at it critically: 'I want elephants on my wallpaper.'

'But there are elephants everywhere. They're just hiding behind the leaves,' I answered, treacherously, and left him looking for them.

'I can't see the elephants,' he said next morning.

'Keep looking,' I answered, protecting the wallpaper. 'Just because you can't see them doesn't mean they're not there.'

Ten years too late, I apologise for that. Of course I should have changed the wallpaper. But, amazingly, he did not bear a grudge. 'Hopeful' even at that moment, he kept looking. He gave me the benefit of the doubt that there might be elephants there, in hiding.

Max's arrival forced me to change in ways I would never have done had too much not been asked of me. Had all our lives gone on as they 'ought' to have done, had I had children of my own, I would now be experiencing all the normal confusions of a parent: where do I stop and where does my son start? As it is I now feel about Max as a person might who wakes up to find a bluebird in their garden. As long as it stays I lay out the best bread and hope that it will keep returning. But since the bird is not 'mine', when it goes I will be left with no recrimination, only gratitude.

A Virtuous Woman

MICHAEL BYWATER

Michael Bywater was brought up in Nottinghamshire and now lives in London. He is a columnist for the Independent on Sunday. *His book* Godzone *will be published in 1996. He has one daughter but lives with a bad yellow-eyed woman and a big harpsichord, and has only just realised that he is not immortal after all.*

Emotionally labile, speechless unsocialized dwarf seeks unpaid carer. Lifetime commitment sought. Must be comfortable with incontinence, egocentricity, insomnia, sudden inexplicable outbursts of rage, etc. Initially on call twenty-four hours daily. Will be required to provide, on demand, food, clothing, physical affection, basic grounding in life skills, numeracy, literacy, treats, friends, holidays, clothing and shelter for advertiser, who undertakes to increase radically in size during course of engagement. Remuneration: lineaments of satisfied desire initially, which successful applicant may choose to interpret as reciprocated affection. Subsequent compensation to be provided on a sliding

scale including resentment, sulking, defiance, embarrassment
and unacceptable personal habits. N.B. The successful applicant
for this post will be expected to take full blame for any disap-
pointments, failures or anxieties arising in later life.

Well; you wouldn't reply, would you? You wouldn't write in.
Of course you wouldn't. But that's the deal. That's probably
the *best* deal, as good as you could hope for. At least you're left
in the dark for a while. Imagine if there were a Truth in
Advertising deal for the unborn. *Genocidal warmonger seeks lov-*
ing Mum. There would still be applicants. *Aaaah. He's only*
little. I can save him. All he needs is some TLC.

It might yet happen. In the long-running case of Nature v.
Nurture, the evidence is coming out more and more on
Nature's side. Scientists – *feh!* – have identified powerful
hereditary predispositions to schizophrenia, burglary, alco-
holism, depression, mathematical ability, arthritis and sexual
orientation. Give them fifty years maximum and they'll be
able to tell from a genetic assay in the first trimester.
Congratulations, ma'am; it's a chartered accountant. It's a gay
Territorial Army major with a boozer's nose and a wonky hip. It's a
clumsy recidivist on a ten-year stretch. It's a Mother's Boy.
Congratulations.

In the face of such a prospect, it seems better not to know.
When I was a proper journalist, I used, in the way of daily
trade, to encounter horrors. Not just the big, dramatic horrors, but the sad, quiet, desperate ones too. The drunk in the
gutter, everything lost and gone. The little failure who could-
n't understand why. The old lady whom nobody came to see
any more. The suicide, dead of an overdose in his company

car. Small-time contractors in the bankruptcy court. The junkie whore, looks gone, skin like paper, sitting outside my local tube station begging, her eyes huge and vertiginous, not because they were so nearly filled with despair and shame, but because of the tiny flame of hope and pride they still held.

It was hard to be detached; hard to go back to the office and write them up, great story, arseholes, losers, fuck 'em, right? I didn't have what it takes. I was a sissy; kept imagining their early days, when they were little, when there was one person, at least, who was pleased to see them; who loved them and smiled at them and fed them and was enchanted with everything they did.

There's no redemption there, not in this harsh world, but it seemed as if there should be; as if having been loved once could lift the suicide from his despair, the bankrupt from his ruin, the hooker from the degradation of the ten-quid trick. And politicians, too: financiers, hamburger executives, corporate hatchet-men, privatisers, Quango overlords, tricksy lawyers, dogmatists, demographers, all the grunting worshippers of the Tory profit-idol: they too should somehow be magically transformed, if you could say of them, like Andrew Aguecheek, 'They were adored once, too.'

Well; what can we say that isn't nonsense? That their mothers may have loved them, but they turned out bad? Or that their mothers didn't love them enough, or loved them too much, which is *why* they turned out bad? No. All you can really say is: their mothers loved them; they turned out bad. No speculative conjunction. We can see the effect, but the cause escapes us.

*

Ever since we stopped pretending to be quite so terribly sure about God, men have been mining motherhood as the fount and origin of life and its troubles. Everything we don't understand about ourselves, everything we dislike, our faults, the unfairness of life, the evils of humanity, the crippling habits we can't quite overcome, our drinking, our sloth, our shyness, our difficulties with women, our emotional illiteracy, our failure to *connect*: all these we lay, like bailiffs' papers and threats to sue, at the door of our mothers. We consult our shrinks. We re-enact our early lives for soft-voiced counsellors. We no longer say, with Job, 'Man is born to sorrow as the sparks fly upward', preferring instead Philip Larkin's celebrated line about Mum and Dad (but mostly Mum). And we forget the second stanza, which lifts it from its commonly accorded status of a universal whine; the stanza which begins: 'But they were fucked up in their turn . . .' Sons and Mothers? Indeed; and how easy it would be, for this son at least, to write about his mother like a theatre critic reviewing a particular actor's interpretation of a universal role. And how dull; how distorted; how like a child's drawing: two-dimensional, unshaded, done from memory and wrong in each particular. I remember a *Punch* cartoon: the first frame showed a group of kindergarten children, drawing Mummy; we were looking over the shoulder of one child whose drawing was predictably inept and grotesque. In the second frame, the children were piling out of school and there were the mothers, waiting. Among them was Mummy: face-on in outline, great distorted snaggle-tooth head, 3B pencil hair, stick body and insect limbs.

Were I to sit here and type out my picture of Mummy, you

wouldn't recognise her if you met her. You'd be expecting the cartoon at the gate. You'd be expecting a creature of alarming and volcanic mood-swings, tyrannical and marshmallow-soft by turns, one moment two vast and trunkless legs of stone, the next a gay icon, Schiaparelli-scented in a New Look evening dress; now murmuring and cooing, now roaring like frenzy at my sins. It would be like trying to map a country from 20,000 feet: only the highest peaks would stand out, and only the deepest valleys; the rest would be levelled by sheer distance into a featureless plain.

But that's not what you would see if you met. You'd see the small complexities of her landscape: a stranger at whose inner geography you could probably not even guess. You might never see the mountains or the canyons. And you certainly would never see Audrey Jean Bywater, née Price, born Newport, Monmouthshire, in such-and-such a year; you'd never see her complete, illuminated by the infinitely subtle chiaroscuro of a human existence lived on this planet. We barely know ourselves; every other life is a foreign country; you would no more know hers than I do. If you could see her through my eyes, she wouldn't look . . . *human* at all.

There's a dream which most writers share: to delineate so precisely and completely an imagined individual life that not only would the telling of it become complete in itself, without the need for the usual mechanisms of fiction – plot, structure, narrative voice, point of view – but the person so described would somehow step out of the pages to conduct a real existence. It never happens. We may tell each other that 'the characters are taking on a life of their own', but they never do. They can't. So some give up early and turn to biography, hoping that, even if they can never create life, they may be able to reanimate the dead, or breathe a human spark into the arid moribundity of a Big Name or celeb. Others – Americans are much given to this – endlessly re-tell their own story in the hope, perhaps, of making good that very lack of perceived reality in their lives which drove them in the first place to the pen, the haemorrhoids and the midnight oil.

And even if we can glimpse the truth of another's life, it's hard to set it down. We demand to read about *characters*; or we demand plot, conflict, incident and drama. The telling of an ordinary life, lived under simple domestic lighting according to the uncelebrated virtues, is too homely and homogenised a brew for our modern, excitable tastes; like Scottish food or sensible shoes, it fails to titillate. We need proof that what we are reading about is worth our attention; which is why television producers, existing to deliver up viewers to advertisers, feed us endless stories about policemen and doctors. We *need* policemen; we *need* doctors; we need them to tell us when something is evil or threatens our lives.

Audrey Jean Bywater, née Price, born Newport, Monmouthshire, on such-and-such a date in such-and-such a year. I know some things about her; I possess the Dead Sea Scrolls of her life: fragments of detail, some important, some trivial, jumbled and incomplete. Her mother was Lilian: Devon and Irish blood, mostly; rural on one side, laughing-mad Celtic seafaring on the other. Her father was Ivor:

Gloucestershire yeoman stock, roast-beef people who chewed every mouthful a hundred times; every word, every gesture, every action. Four sibs, all younger. Barbara, fiery, a glint in her eye, who became a nurse, married Neville, raised her sons, spends her retirement years travelling and wondering about getting thin again. Marion, thin all along, married thin, dark, piratical Brian, moved to Bournemouth and then to Tenby. Lilian, a soft-featured, smudgy, peaches-and-cream peach of a girl: married her George, a big, ruddy, easy-going man, a man for Rugby Union and decent beer, and expanded into happy, ample motherhood. Young Ivor: followed Old Ivor into Whitehead's steelworks, went into the pottery business, lived in Poole, known in all the old pubs of that old pub town but a man of mystery, his inner life secret and self-sufficient as an oyster.

And my mother. She wasn't my mother then; she was Jean, the eldest child, sharing the child-rearing with *her* mother. The early photographs of her show a determined, fearless tomboy: a mop of bobbed auburn hair, bright eyes, a firm-set jaw; skinned knees and barked shins beneath the skirt you'd bet she hated wearing. Or did she? And did these photographs exist? Have I seen them, or made them up from what I know and what I imagine? I don't know. I could ask her; but that would be cheating.

All the same, I know that the photographs are real, even if they don't exist; I know they hold the terrible poignancy of any picture of any child who has grown up to adulthood. This was her, then, when she had no idea that this was how things were going to turn out. It doesn't matter *how* things turned out, good or bad; it's just that they *have* turned out; so many questions answered, so many choices made, so many turnings taken. When I look at my daughter, I want her to be all the things she could be, all of them, but I know that it's impossible. It's a leaky, comfortless boat, and the fact that we're all in it together is no help at all.

There don't seem to be any photographs in my mental album between that one and her young womanhood. The war came. She went to college, in Portsmouth, and fell in love with a naval officer. He was a regular feature in my childhood: the Man She Should Have Married. Not all the time; just when my father was playing up. 'You make me *sick*!' she would cry. 'My God, I should have married . . .' But what was his name? I can't remember. And was he the one whom she left because spittle collected at the corners of his mouth when he talked? Or was he the one she left because he kept his change in a little leather purse and always knew, to the half-penny, how much was in there? I can't remember.

Then she came to Nottingham to teach. Met my father: came to his surgery one day with a sprained ankle. Once the ankle healed, my father struck her off his list and asked her out. He'd had it, poor bugger, and I can see why, because there's another photograph now. All the energy of the tomboy, but come into full bloom. Thick wavy hair; those eyes; the ivory skin; the figure. The picture said: trouble. It said: tempestuous. It said: worth it, though. My Daddy, normally a quiet, contained man, went into testosterone meltdown. She was engaged to someone else at the time; she told him so; he removed the ring from her finger and said, 'Not any more you're not,' and threw it down a drain. Or sold it and kept the money. Or something. I can't remember. He had a Stetson hat, which he wore on their first date. 'I'm not going out with you if you wear that hat,' she said. I don't know whether he kept the hat on or not, but it's something she still remembers: 'I said to Daddy, "I'm not going out with you if you wear that hat." It was a ten-gallon hat. You know. One of those awful . . . ten-gallon hats.' 'It was a good hat; a Stetson,' says Daddy. 'Mummy hated it.' 'It was awful,' she says.

And so they got married. They bought a little house and wanted children straight away, but it didn't happen. It took several years, and in those days they didn't have the array of tests and counselling we have now; you took your chances, kept trying and hoped for the best; and, if not, bad luck.

But their luck held, if you can call it luck. After a vicious pregnancy which left my mother knackered and gasping for survival like a gaffed fish, the world population was increased by me. I suppose my mother was pretty damn pleased to see me, but at that stage I was too busy being pretty damn pleased to see myself, strutting and bellowing like a little Gauleiter at the centre of my own wonderful, solipsistic one-man show even to be aware of the feelings of others, let alone pay attention to them . . . and by the time I began to notice whether or not my mother really *was* pleased to see me and have me around, she had stopped being quite so unequivocally enchanted.

Or perhaps I had stopped being quite so unequivocally enchanting. We do. Children do. Small boys, in particular, do, and women tell me that the joy and delight in having produced a male child, something so *different* from them, can in time be partially or even wholly overwhelmed by the sheer horror of having produced . . . something so *different*. I suppose it has to happen; we *are* different, and must learn to become so. Shrinks tell us that this is the primal psychic wound, the separation of the son from the mother; the scar never heals, and that's why men are in so many ways so horrible. But men aren't that bad, and shrinks talk balls.

I can't place the moment this happened, the moment the enchantment began to wear off. The world comes into focus gradually when you hunt back through your memories, and the earliest ones are wholly idyllic. She was always there, without fail, to pick me up, comfort me, feed me, croon at me, so predictably and reliably so that I simply never noticed. She had a little car, a baby Austin called Ovo after its numberplate, and I remember going on journeys with her – probably just a few miles, to see friends, but they seemed like Odysseys – and she would sing to me, usually a song from *The King and I*:

> Getting to know you
> Getting to know all about you
> Getting to like you,
> Hoping that you like me

. . . and suddenly I have to stop typing because my eyes have filled with tears and the screen has gone out of focus and *I* have gone out of focus; what has come *into* focus is Audrey Jean Bywater, née Price, born Newport, Monmouthshire, on such-and-such a date in such-and-such a year, and here she is, tootling along in her little car with her little son and she's happy and she loves him so much she has to sing. And he's me. He's *me*.

★

Unconditional love? Don't talk to me about unconditional love. We've buggered that one up, too, with a little help from the shrinks. That's another one the shrinks have got their hands on. There's the primal psychic wound, and there's unconditional love. We're all seeking it. That's what we want from our relationships. Well . . . *nuts*. There's only one place you get unconditional love, only one direction in which it flows: from parent to child. That's it. Anyone who wants unconditional love from another adult would be all the better for a good, hard smack. And another thing: unconditional love doesn't imply unconditional liking, or unconditional approval or unconditional *anything*.

Why am I saying this? I'm saying it for my benefit. I'm saying it for me. Not for you. You probably know it already. Me, I've only just found out. Oh, I've had my *suspicions* – had them for several years now, since I was thirty-nine years old – but they've only just this second been confirmed.

I could have saved myself some trouble, had I been able to distinguish between love and approval, and between disapproval and sound advice vehemently expressed. I could have saved myself time and expense, all that money spent on showing off, trinkets and accessories, status symbols which quite possibly symbolised *someone*'s status, but not my own. All that time spent tangling myself in a knot, finding women disposed to disapprove of me and trying to win them round. All that anxiety. All that investment in learning how to be an asshole.

It's not that mothers possess terrible, limitless power that causes trouble. It's that children are . . . *children*. Rebellious, defiant, unable to make distinctions; emotionally illiterate, desperately insecure. When I take to my couch to drool over my sorrows and imagine myself an emotionally damaged person, I brood over terrible injustices like the time when, aged nine, I scrawled marks of interpretation all over my copy of Handel's *Harmonious Blacksmith*. Changing my mind a few days later, and resenting that I had defaced the score, I stole another one on my way up to my piano lesson in the studios above Clement Pianos in Market Street. On the way out, I realised that I would be unable to account for my having *two* copies, so stuffed the defaced one up the chimney under the astonished eye of a piano tuner, whose fixed and startled gaze I took to be evidence of what I then believed was the blindness obligatory in his trade. He told my piano teacher; she rang my mother; my mother asked me what on earth I had been thinking of. Had I gone *mad*? Could I please *explain*?

An injustice; a withdrawal of unconditional love; a deep psychic wound? Hell, yes; you bet it was. Just like the day she chased me round the sitting-room brandishing a shrimping net and threatening me with the police. And why? What had I done? Nothing. Nothing apart from embezzling my Bob-a-Job Week money and spending it on sweets, a packet of five Woodbines and a copy of *Fiesta* magazine featuring a photospread of Cyd Charisse, with whom – and, in particular, with whose thirty-six-inch inside legs – I consummated my passion behind the abandoned reservoir on Mickelborough Hill before burying my beloved under a stone and creeping home, my illicit lusts incandescent in every pore. A shrimping net! Threats of the police! Was that reasonable?

Was it reasonable to be told to watch my bloody neck when I blew up the chemistry laboratory *three times* in one class (hydrogen; bunsen flame applied to asbestos sheet; hydrogen again to make sure it wasn't an experimental error the first time)? Was it reasonable to be told, when every teacher commented to her that I was a lazy bugger, that I might consider making a little more effort or else the shit would hit the fan? Was it reasonable of her, when she came up to Cambridge to visit me and I arrived over an hour late, drunk, unshaven, wearing eye make-up, green nail polish, a black velvet cloak, with my hair dyed black and a gold ring in my ear; was it *reasonable* of her to *burst into tears*? Was it? *Was it?*

Of course it was, and, merciful heavens, I must have been a *bugger*. I think I started being a bugger when, aged six, I discovered the power of fiction. 'I've got,' I said to Anne Morrell, whom I loved, 'a mouse in my pocket.' It wasn't quite Mae West's line, but it did the trick. She gazed at me with admiration and, that afternoon, asked if she could sit next to me in class. But our teacher, Miss Foster, had overheard, and grassed me up. 'Why,' said my mother, 'did you say you had a mouse in your pocket?' Again, not an unreasonable question, but one I found unanswerable. I know now that a writer is someone who, having made his bed, must lie about it; but then I just shuffled, grunted, and picked at the good old psychic wound.

Thereafter, I plied my vocation at every opportunity. It must have been indescribably bewildering for this straightforward young woman (and, when I look back, she seems impossibly young, neat, pretty and hopeful in her A-line skirt) to find she had brought forth from her diligent and well-ordered life – from her own personal *uterus*, for heaven's sake – a fantasist, a maverick, a *weirdo* who loathed sports, refused to countenance teamwork of any sort, showed off, told obvious and pointless lies (once, aged seven, driving through Warwickshire, I pointed to a man on a tractor in a distant field, no more than a dot, and said, 'I *know* that man,' at which my mother's safety-valve blew and she hissed: '*Don't* talk such *rubbish*. Why do you *say* these things?' – another psychic wound) and refused or was unable to explain his behaviour in any particular.

It must have been a bit like finding out you have worms. In my mind's eye, I can see her, watching me when I wasn't looking, wondering what on earth was going on in my head; whether I was some kind of cuckoo, or if it was just a phase, and, if so, how the hell long a phase could last and still be called a phase.

Even when she was in her twenties, my mother knew – and still knows - what she stood for and why she was there. They were uncomplicated things: a secure home, her family well-cared for, her children encouraged to reach their best potential. Food on the table, warmth and comfortable beds, the sound and ancient virtues of honesty, reliability, security. Grandchildren in due course, and the prospect of great-grandchildren and her line going down through the generations. Modest but serious and grown-up ambitions; but somewhere in that earnest dreamscape, the laughing tomboy and the shining-eyed young beauty got lost and entangled.

I didn't help, of course. I grew into a turbulent adolescent, inhabiting a strange universe which I was both unable and unwilling to communicate. Both my father and mother were broad-church middlebrows, but my own brow was not merely high but ineffable, and from its lofty peaks they seemed posi-tively Neanderthal. I didn't give a damn for their humane decency, nor did I appreciate the tolerance with which they indulged my obsessions or the kindly and quite genuine attempts they made to understand my exotic tastes: Tudor polyphony, Baroque organ music, avant-garde art, the wilder shores of scientific speculation, outlandish liturgical ceremo-nial so high as to induce anoxia. I hadn't the wisdom or experience to understand that when a parent seeks to learn and share the tastes of a child, it is one of the most graceful and charming compliments that can be paid. I had charac-terised them as knuckle-draggers, and, determined to keep them that way, shut them out from my life. This, I think, is a common experience; but it must have hurt them badly. I know that my mother believed I was ashamed of her, but I don't think I was. I think it went further than that, and I was ashamed of *having parents at all*. It somehow didn't seem appropriate to the egregious persona I had constructed for myself. In retrospect, I think I was round the bend.

And so I shut them out; and could indulge the luxury of having parents who Did Not Understand Me, though what I would have done with parents who *did* understand me, I do not know. Probably shaped up a bit and stopped being such a pain in the arse.

Now, of course, it seems extraordinarily cruel. I look back at that pretty girl singing to her child in her little car, and I curse myself for the degree of happiness I denied her. But, wading about in a thick mud of self-obsession for much of my life, I gave it no thought until recently. Though I do recall one summer evening, the year I finished university. I was pleasantly drunk; it was a lovely evening, and I was so full of the sense of possibility and hope and things having not yet . . . *turned out*, that I rang my mother and, hopelessly unable to explain in any coherent detail the tremendous surge of joy at my very existence and all the things that had been done for me, I simply told her, in a slightly slurred voice, that I loved her. And you could probably deduce a lot about my behaviour up to that point by the fact that her immediate reaction was to wonder whether I was all right.

Watching me grow up, watching me live the first part of my adult life, must in many ways have been a nightmare for her, and she must at times have wondered when she was going to wake up and find us back at the beginning again, starting over at one of those moments of perfect felicity: leading me through the park on my tricycle, in my Christopher Robin hat and coat, my gloves threaded through my sleeves with elastic; taking me, two years old, on the train down to Newport, to show me off to her parents; teaching me to read; standing with me in the bow-window of the drawing-room one summer afternoon when the sky darkened early and we scampered home just before the storm broke and the dugout flooded and the whole world was suffused with the smell of wet earth.

Sometimes, in despair, she would cry, saying, 'I don't know where I went wrong.' I thought it was over-dramatising; a self-indulgence; but now I think she was telling the truth. She *didn't* know; she thought that here she had a son who despised her, and that it must be her fault. What she really had was a son who, for reasons I do not understand even now, had built himself an almost impregnable cage and was unable to do much other than rattle the bars.

The storm broke no more than three years ago. Finally exhausted by the rickety, Heath Robinson vehicle of my existence and its constant derailments – financial crises, emotional crises, infidelity, divorce, bankruptcy, doomed affairs and the cycle showing every sign of cranking up for yet another revolution – I started to look at the patterns of my life, and there was one in particular that I couldn't face down. I needed to confront it and find out how it had come about. 'I always felt,' I said, 'that nothing I could do was ever enough. That I had to be perfect, or I was nothing. That being loved and accepted was conditional on how I performed.'

Shrink-speak, and glib to boot. Foreseeing the consequences of one's words or actions can sometimes be unhelpful. If I had known what a tumult of grief I would bring down, I would never have spoken; and that would have been a loss. 'I am just devastated,' she said, and it was neither an exaggeration nor a ruse to make me retract. It was as though I had pulled the ground from beneath her. I thought she would never stop crying. 'If I'd *known* you felt like that,' she said. 'I can't forgive myself for making you think that; it's awful, it's the most awful thing; I loved you, you've no idea, it never *mattered* what you did, I just always hoped you'd be able to do what you wanted, to be happy, oh God, I never *knew* . . .'

Even while my mind was up to its old tricks, trying to persuade me that this was all a device to make me feel bad about a legitimate complaint, even while I was telling myself that Portnoy would never have Complained, to our infinite loss, had he allowed himself to fall for this emotional blackmail, I knew that what she was saying was true. She had loved me all along, and I had constructed this torture-chamber for myself, but it had not been my fault. I had descended into the oldest trap of humanity, and had noticed only the bad things, never the good. Now I was free.

For a couple of years beforehand, my mother had been under the weather: tiring easily, off her food, lacking in energy. She had had all the tests, but nothing clear had emerged. Last year, though, they did a test they could, and should, have done much sooner. They found that she had contracted hepatitis-C from a blood transfusion thirty-seven years ago, when she was pregnant with my sister. If they had diagnosed it earlier, she might have been fine. But by then, it had caused severe liver damage. She was put on devastating doses of powerful chemotherapeutic drugs which seem to have arrested the progress of the disease, but at the cost of severe side-effects.

She has carried on throughout with extraordinary stoicism and resilience, but it has been a cruel blow. It's saddening to see a woman with such force of life and will reduced to a near-invalid; but I am glad that both of us perhaps now understand a little more of the misconceptions which caused us both so much silly, unnecessary pain. We talk a lot now, and we have indeed had another chance. When she tells me how much she loved playing with me and looking after me when I was little, it's almost as though we were there again, and all the damage of the years is undone. What I find surprising is that when I hear these things, I don't think of myself any more, nor do I see her just as my mother, who may not after all live for ever; but instead I see a laughing tomboy, an auburn beauty, a happy young mother singing to her child, a grown woman proud of her son, a doting grandmother, an old lady bearing illness bravely: all at once, in her continuum: Audrey Jean Bywater, née Price, born Newport, Monmouthshire, on such-and-such a date in such-and-such a year, a virtuous woman who gave me my life.

S t r e n g t h   t h r o u g h G e n t l e n e s s

JENNY CRADDOCK

Dr Jenny Craddock lives and works in London. She is mother to Sam, Ben and Emily, foster-mother to Chris, George, Linda and Peter, and psychotherapist to many.

When Sam walked into his grandparents' home on that spring evening I was astonished. How had he known to come, to come to Yorkshire and to come then? Had we somehow drawn on that invisible silver communicating thread? I had not asked Sam to drive all that way at the end of his long working day. Grandpa's illness had been so swift that none of us, except maybe Sam, knew how little time remained. Grandpa had impeccable manners and was never one to impose. Even so ill, he apologised to us for his modest needs. If there is such a thing as a loving leaving, I believe his was. As Sam walked towards the bed, his grandpa reached out his oh so skinny arms and drew Sam's head down to his chest. He held Sam there for the longest time. It seemed to us, looking on, that this brave man was passing his very life-force to his grandson.

For Sam's grandpa David was a hero. He had medals to show for his bravery though he never showed them. On 19 September 1944, having survived the North African campaign and the horrific battles in Italy for the capture of Monte Cassino, David crossed the River Ausa with B Squadron and the 48th Highlanders. One account states that 'they were subjected to a merciless pounding'. Heroism comes at a high price. David's cost him his handsome young face. Over the years that followed, at Queen Victoria Hospital, East Grinstead, the brilliant plastic surgeons Dr Ross Tilley and Dr McIndoe 'reconstructed' David's face. Many of the wounded young men in David's ward didn't even tell their families they were alive. During their convalescence, David with a group of other 'guinea pigs' went on an outing to see *The Tommy Trinder Show*. At Victoria Station, the ticket collector said, 'They shouldn't be allowed out like that.'

David was a very important influence in Sam's young life and Sam loved him. Grandpa and Grandma lived with us in Hampstead, so Sam was able to spend time with them and enjoy their humour, love and wise counsel. From his grandpa Sam learnt that it is not what you see outside that matters but what a person is within. Heroism is not the sum of the experiences an individual has endured, but what he makes of those experiences. David's courage and bravery were extended far beyond the battlefield to living and working with his damaged face for the rest of his life. It made him a truly gentle man. David taught us all that love is genuine care and concern for one another and the ability to accept one another just the way we are. The true tragedy of Narcissus was that he was so numbed by his own beauty that he was incapable of love.

Sam was my first child, my number one son. My blood group is Rhesus Negative and Sam's, like his father's, is Rhesus Positive, so Sam was meant to be the 'only' one. His Caesarean birth was just months before Anti-D (Rh) immunoglobulin became available to prevent haemolytic disease of the newborn and the distress of exchange blood transfusions.

From his first movements within my womb he amazed me. After the initial separation of his birth, I spent hours marvelling at the miracle of this little one, his sturdy limbs, tiny fingers, his serene blue eyes, and his adorable smell.

He didn't come with instructions – so when he cried, I would anxiously try to interpret the source of his distress and gradually learnt his ways and needs. Raised as I was to use my two ears, two eyes and one mouth in proportion, I was comfortable with this quiet communication I think we are still quite quiet people who prefer to listen.

It was Sam who interpreted David's puzzling last signals to me. A round 'O' with his thumb and forefinger to his ear meant, Sam explained, that he was 'O.K. here [ear].' Thank you, Sam.

From the moment of his birth, loving my child meant to me continually standing back and beside but 'letting go' - from sitting up, to walking, to running, riding a bike, swimming, kicking a football, climbing trees, and school. Given a choice, I think I would have preferred that Sam did not swing from a pulley between two telegraph poles at the adventure playground, climb mountains, soar over ski-jumps or steer his canoe through white waters, but these Herculean tasks seemed essential elements in his rite of passage towards manhood. I struggled to practise Goethe's teaching: 'If I love you, what business is it of yours?'

As my role of 'mother' included driving to and from school and to his chosen after-school events, I was quite closely involved in Sam's young life. It was usually in the car that he would share with me his ideas and developing philosophies. I particularly enjoyed these times with him as I felt that guilt common to all working mothers who have to pack their 'mothering hours' into tight spaces. Sam's father was ill and out of work for many of Sam's young years. Sam was just two years old when he stood as still as a little sentry beside me in a side-ward at University College Hospital watching Father Alan Cheales administer the last rites to Sam's dying father. The kindly, white-robed Dominican friar leant towards little Sam and told him to be very brave as Malcolm, his father, was soon to die. 'No,' said Sam. 'He is not.' Sam was right.

Malcolm had contracted septicaemia while he was filming the Mardi Gras carnival in Trinidad. He survived the usually lethal septic shock, an allergic reaction to the antibiotics and the surgery, but recurrent bouts of osteomyelitis meant several returns to hospital.

Those years were hard. My own recollections are obscured by the fog of fatigue in which I seemed to live. Sam remembers the arrival of his little brother, Ben, who seemed to Sam then, although not now, superfluous to requirements. Sam recalls the days spent with their dependable daily minder, Ada. No one since, he says, has made better chips. On Mondays Ada pushed the big bouncy pram with the boys and her twin girls to the Kentish Town bath-houses. Sam remembers the wonderful smell of the pile of clean linen and his important task of holding the bag of fresh doughnuts for tea on the journey back.

Sam also remembers his days at nursery school as happy days. Andrea Taylor taught him to paint, to draw and to sing. His performances in concerts at Hampstead Hill School helped him grow in confidence and there he was introduced, through learning to read and to write, to the wonderful world of words. Now as then, he usually has a book in a pocket somewhere about his person. Sam made enduring friendships 'at Andrea's', where he learnt that our friends are our true wealth in life.

Sam was heartbroken when we moved house away from his friends Fred and Josh, whose garden backed on to ours. We still arranged to meet up at the adventure playground, but the neighbourly spontaneity was lost. Three essential elements for the happiness of a child are loving, understanding and choosing. I do so hope Sam felt loved. He was without doubt a courageous, friendly and loving child.

How much he was able to understand of his father's illness and the effect this had on our lives is unclear to me. We tried to explain but he was so very small then. Difficult decisions, like the house move, were made which were not of his choosing. Unable to comprehend the reasons for the sale, Sam expressed animosity to the incoming house purchasers rather than protest to us that he did not want to move. I also worked for the two of us, both day and night, while Malcolm recovered. Malcolm was self-employed and we soon exhausted our modest insurance cover. I worked on the night-shift at our local hospital and modelled or did what other jobs I could find during the day. I had little difficulty in keeping still for the camera but great difficulty in keeping awake.

I felt great sadness and shame that, inevitably, the separations made Sam anxious. He was just three years old on that awful, unforgettable night at Lawn Road Hospital when I was working with the 'crash' team, trying to resuscitate an elderly patient's failing heart. I looked up and to my dismay saw little Sam standing in the ward doorway holding Night Sister's hand. Our patient was in the first bed on the left side of the long ward and, in our haste, we had only drawn the curtains on two sides. Sam was exposed to a full and probably very frightening view of our labours. I was giving heart massage as other members of the team put up drips and gave the appropriate drugs while the anaesthetist intubated our patient and administered oxygen.

Sam, I later learnt as I tucked him back into bed, had woken in the middle of the night feeling lonely and, as the household slept, put on his dressing-gown and slippers, climbed out of a window and then heroically walked half a mile and across a major road to the hospital.

'I wondered where you were', he said. 'Why were you thumping that poor man? That's mean.'

And I felt *so* mean.

However, for most of his early years Sam too wanted to be a doctor, ophthalmic surgery being the area which interested him most. At the hospital I would show him how an electron microscope worked, and he could calculate visual fields at nine years old.

My relationship with Sam changed as he changed. Through puberty, the time for hugs and kisses diminished. In the process of becoming a man, Sam modelled himself on the best qualities of his father. He no longer spoke of medicine. His homework prevented him from coming to the hospital, and anyway we had reached that galling phase when I could only offer help with French homework. Sam had managed a balance between being a very spiritual individual and yet an outgoing and amusing one. He worked very hard and his studies won him deserved academic success. He also played hard and, as captain of football, water-polo and basketball, he developed his leadership skills.

Sam loved the magic of the movies which took his father away from home to exotic locations for months on end. His father made the dreams of so many talented young people come to life on screen. Sam understood something then which took me many more years to learn. You can work hard on a one-to-one basis and perhaps make some small difference to the lives of others, but if you dare to put your message on to the screen you reach millions.

Sam first worked for a video post-production company, and when I say worked, he really worked. He worked as many hours as, possibly more than, a junior house officer. He was desperate to prove that he had this job on his own merits and not because of his father's success as a producer. To my immense relief and gratitude, Ken Russell's son Xavier took Sam aside after one Tottenham Hotspur game and explained to Sam the nature of envy in the world of the beautiful people. 'You could work 168 hours a week,' Xavier told him, 'and people would *still* say you got the job because your father is who he is.'

Sam then began to learn about pre-production and the

making of films. He was pleased and excited to be chosen to work as assistant director to the very talented Stephen Whittaker on *Closing Numbers*, starring Jane Asher. In my opinion, this film is one of the most courageous and moving works to be shown on British television. Appropriately, it is the young son in the story who is the real hero and brings his father back home.

After that film, Sam took his paternal grandpa back to Italy to thank the brave people who had hidden him as an escaped prisoner-of-war. Sam made up a bed in his Defender Land-Rover for Grandpa to rest during the long overland journey. Sam understood the need to go back and say thank you, before it is too late.

Then, recognising that you can do nothing about what other people will enviously say or think − so why worry about it? − Sam worked for arduous years on his father's productions of the Sharpe hero-soldier stories set during the time of the Peninsular War and filmed in Russia and lately in Turkey. Sam has a quiet, brave authority which enables him to control vast crowds of extras, enlist the cooperation of even quite wayward horses, and resolve conflicts between crew or cast members with respect and courtesy.

Recently, stopped at the traffic lights where Queensway joins Westbourne Grove, we saw that the corner pub had emptied its late-night drinkers on to the pavement where a huge and vicious fight was going on. Sam put on his hazard lights, jumped out of his Landy and, to my absolute amazement, stopped the fight and made the crowds disperse. I was astonished.

Sam's little sister, Emily, nine years his junior, has asked me to mention her gratitude to Sam for saving her life. They were skiing in Zermatt when Emily had a fall and was injured. Sam brought her safely down from the mountain and to medical help. Cold, in pain and waiting for him to find her, she had been so afraid. Thank you again, Sam.

Sam is now ready to make the move into his own work and has, unsurprisingly, chosen to film a world little understood and perhaps therefore feared. His subject is the life of the Mozart Estate and what makes a hero in that dangerous place. Although opposite Harrow Road police station, this estate has earned itself a reputation which would make any stranger hesitate to enter. Sam regards the residents of this place not as depressed and dependent, pushers and poor, but as a tight-knit community with their own loyalties and laws, heroes and oppressors. He is working with them to write their stories as they wish them told. Ferocious yet often funny, these tales will, Sam hopes, help us to respect, as he does, their fight to survive and to overcome their obstacles with dignity. 'Not what you see from the outside, but what is within.' Grandpa would be proud, I feel.

Buddhist philosophy tells us that a child is not our 'possession' but a vulnerable soul lodging with us for a duration. I also believe that C-minus is the top mark for motherhood. Each generation strives to build faster, cleaner planes, trains and automobiles and to be better parents than their own. Without this margin for error, there can be no growth, no development. However hard we may try to be good parents, we do, and we must, inevitably fall short of the ideal. If we can accept our shortcomings we can, in an imperfect world, respect and accept one another, just as we are. I think perhaps this acceptance – without 'blame' or 'fault', 'should' or 'ought' – is what love is.

My favourite photograph of Sam shows him handing his younger brother's other wellington boot to Ben, who is up to his knees in mud. It sums up their relationship and, in many ways, ours too. Sam is always there, courageous, quiet and calm, interpreting needs and offering appropriate help. In the mould of his grandfather, a truly gentle man.

The Quality
of Mercy

DIRAN ADEBAYO

*Diran Adebayo, of Nigerian descent, was born in
London in 1968. He studied law at Oxford and has
since written for newspapers ranging from the* Voice *to
the* Daily Express. *His debut novel,* Some Kind of
Black, *was the first novel to win the Saga Prize. Diran
is currently working on his second novel.*

26 / 6 / 89 2:00 a.m.

*Fine Young Cannibals: 'She Drives Me Crazy'. In Ian's
place, v. wrecked. About to go thru' one of my more fateful days
of my life. Splitting up with my parents? going home to deliver
the 'big blow'. (I think today, job I/V in Kensington, i.e. get
a flat, earn some money etc.)
God, it's such a big day today.*

Those lines, dashed into my diary that night, proved to be
horribly ironic. I was, indeed, splitting with my parents, but
not in the way I was plotting. Earlier that night, unknown to

me, on the other side of London, my mother had died. Suddenly, of an asthma attack. She was fifty-two.

When I look back at those lines I am struck by two things. First, by the fact that my mother's passing coincided with my last day at college. (I was staying over at a friend's and was due to come home in the morning.) Education of the children was at the top of my family's agenda, an all-enveloping imperative, and so it made a cruel, perverse kind of sense that she should die as her youngest child completed his studies.

The second thing that strikes me is the way in which I so easily included my mother in what was really a day of reckoning with my Dad. We had had minor spats over my future, in the way that fathers and teenage sons do, and yet actions that I contemplated in response were wont to affect the two of them.

The atmosphere of the home – its rigour, its discipline, its severity – seemed to me then to be based on male organising principles. Even if my mother was frequently responsible for its implementation, the agenda seemed set by my father. My mother's personality, in comparison, seemed muted and diminished. I suspected, then, that we could only take our relationship to the free and frank plane that I craved after I'd left the house. Over and above the terrible loss I feel is one persistent frustration: now I will never know what she was truly like.

My parents came over from Lagos, Nigeria, in the mid-60's. They emigrated to further their careers, their studies – science, in my Dad's case – and to ensure that their children could seize the untold opportunities available in the mother-country. My mother had won a civil service scholarship and came to take up a post at the Department of the Environment, where she stayed, in a PA-type position, until her death. By the time that I came along, my folks had a brood of five to contend with. No doubt my parents understood that things were going to be hard for them in order, eventually, to be easier for us. Still, they could scarcely have anticipated that things would be so unrelentingly uphill, and the good life – my father had been a successful journalist in Nigeria, and their marriage had made the gossip columns – gone for so long, as we waited for our material blessings to rise.

We used to live off Green Lanes in Harringay, north London. We moved, after a family bereavement, to Wood Green, down the road from Tottenham. Wood Green was a kinda peculiar area. A number of black folk, Caribbeans mainly, jostled with a greater number of white C2 types. The parents were the sort who voted Mrs Thatcher in on the regular, while their offspring were seduced by black intonations and street styles. There was a bingo hall and, further up the High Road, towards Arnos Grove, a bunch of business-minded Greeks and Cypriots lived in a community we called Little Athens. You could shoot pool in little clubs around Turnpike Lane, and Jah Shaka, a great dub reggae name, played a popular dance behind the local library – although we children were not encouraged to hang out with the locals. The area was as cosmopolitan as much of north London then, but had a certain bleakness, no doubt partly because of the lack, in the early days at least, of shops.

Shops were a big deal. It seems that my Mum was forever doing or dealing with the shopping. The old Jones Bros. on

Holloway Road for clothes, and any number of food places that have an incantatory effect on me to this day. Blackstock Road and the market just off Petticoat Lane for chicken, small peppers, dried fish and Nigerian goodies, Stroud Green Road for grey mullet. And the names of the joints of meat she brought back! Topside, silverside. . . . I still go to markets to buy meat just so I can recite these names to butchers who know.

Mum would come from work via shopping, and still be on the go. Dumping her bags, frying and seasoning, dashing upstairs to change, bathroom door open, then back to the kitchen.

Soon the room would be full of that particular tickling fog of peppers, onions and spices: a pall acrid enough to fell the casual visitor, but one in which my mother beavered away unperturbed. And one that was instantly comforting to all of us. It meant that Mommy was around.

No doubt the business of food plays a big part in most family households. For a home whose touchstones were order and 'no time for larking about', this ritual carried even greater weight. My Mum had to be home by a certain time in order to have the food on the table at a certain time. Her unstinting daily routine thus embodied, in a certain sense, the aspirational ideal of this orthodox West African household. Not that we voiced it in those terms, but we all certainly acknowledged that Mommy was the glue that held us together. In a home where people went about their duties, and open discussion of the real domestic dynamics just didn't go on, my mother was the key conduit of family communication and vital information.

She was the one figure who could move between the lines of father and children, and this quality was relied on by all of us. So she would be the receptacle of the real as opposed to official truths, or at least given as much of the truth as one wished to share with the other side. She was so often the mediator either obliquely, as she conveyed bargaining positions, or sweet glosses on bad news from one camp to the other, or directly, as she pleaded on our behalf if we were being flogged or threatened with other sanctions.

One illustration of this occurred when I was suspended from school. For smoking, drinking, those kinds of things. Anyway, given the grief I had caught for, say, minor domestic infringements, I grew faint just thinking of what would happen when I reached home. I resolved to run away as soon as it became clear I was going to be flogged. When that moment arrived, I was out the house and down the road with a swiftness. My brother and my mother – in her nightie and slippers, poor woman – chased after me. I said that I wouldn't go home unless she could extract a promise from my Dad that I wouldn't be beaten. They walked back and eventually my brother returned to tell me the promise had been won.

But for her presence, I'm sure some extremely ugly incident would have occurred sooner or later in the home. But the way she worked her zones of influence also meant that her loyalties were divided, and sometimes I felt betrayed.

Loyalty is probably the wrong word. She didn't have loyalties, she had objectives, chief of which was to ensure conditions were conducive to us completing our studies. And sometimes she passed on intimacies, or sabotaged my secret plans to further her own conception of how to attain these goals, to my utter exasperation.

When I was a kid, my anger would take the form of running up to her bedroom and emptying the contents of her handbag across the floor. Later, I might abuse her or answer her back, and she would curse (actually curse, as opposed to cuss) me in return.

All the frustrations an 'impotent' child feels towards the order of things I took out brazenly on her, this being who had brought me into this world. Oh, sometimes she would beat me with the wooden spoon, but this was a comparatively puny comeback. More of the time, she could see where the spite was coming from and preferred to act as a sponge-cum-valve, easing and soaking up the pains.

It was a pretty thankless role to play and – I can see now – it took bravery. Back then, I desperately wanted her to be brave, only in the ways I understood Western women in modern-day Britain to be brave. I wanted her to stand up for herself and us, get things changed. Definitely, there were times, when I was down and could see no end in sight, when I wanted her to up and leave and take us with her. And many of my more fractious moments with her were underpinned by a resentment that she would not 'save' us when only she could.

I should explain that I was aware from early on of a burgeoning double consciousness. On the one hand, I was developing a set of European liberal attitudes, percolating from my peers and wider environment. On the other, I had to respond to very different traditions and expectations as far as my African family background was concerned. I juggled these two balls, privileging sometimes one, sometimes the other, but keeping both in sight and trying to muddle through while satisfying both conscience and ego.

The trick of maintaining this double vision successfully is to be very chary with your judgements. Seeing and talking to a mother I cherished about the vows she renewed daily meant that my take on these issues of personal freedom and responsibility could not remain black and white, pardon the pun, for long. She, just through doing the things she did, helped me to a maturer understanding of these matters. She was the mitigating factor then, in that sense, but also more generally, because I was frightened of my father and looked to her for all the mercies.

These mercies ranged from the minor – lying on my behalf, extra playing-time, or midweek top-ups of pocket money in a home where every pound had to be accounted for – to a crucial daily dose of banter and affection.

I would come and interfere with her in the kitchen. A favourite trick was to stack and balance pot after plate on her head as she toiled by the stove, so that she couldn't move without everything crashing down. The more she ignored my routine, the more pots I would place until I heard those distracted, chiding tones: 'Aa-ah, Di-ran! Stop your non-sense!' This nonsense I now inflict on my girlfriend when she's in the kitchen.

Later, when she had retired for the night, and the old man was, say, ensconced in front of the box, I would head upstairs and reason with her in their bedroom. I might try to extract information about family business, or tell her all the sweet things I would do for her when I was grown with money of my own, tease her about something, or else head straight for the cuddle.

I loved this time of the day when she was tired but satisfied.

The chores were done, she had cooked and eaten, she could relax. I liked how her face looked at those times, as she sat propped up on the bed. Serene, soft, unlined and younger than her years, a kind, round-faced prettiness with dimples that I would work on bringing to the surface.

She would most likely call me Ayinla – a middle name and her pet one for me – in these sessions, before trying to cajole me into some course of conduct. Her Bible would lie beside her, adding extra authority to her exhortations.

She read passages from the Good Book frequently before sleeping. In fact, I can barely recall her reading another, which was a shame because she was a big reader in her youth, and her eyes would twinkle at the recollection of the classics she had studied at school. But by the time I was around she was all about Psalms, Proverbs, and the New Testament. Favourite pieces had their page references noted down on slivers of paper that she inserted in her edition.

I often used that Bible as a springboard for emoting about parents and children, rights and duties, love and death, but she was loath to engage me on those levels. She was not interested in all my fancy reasons for not wanting to study medicine, only in whether or not she could change my mind.

The letters she used to send me when I was away at school or college followed a similar pattern. Exhortations to stay on the path chosen, nods to the Scriptures, and frequent referral to my parents' love and devotion to me. I loved the love, and the folds of money that were a godsend in the earlier years, but felt strangely rebuffed that her missives tapped the same tune. I wanted them to show evidence that our relationship was on an arc, tracing an upward curve.

For my offerings on life and the universe were really just attempts to persuade her to open up, and to develop the kind of informed relationship the Western side of me craved. Every now and again, I would throw in a shocking personal titbit to force her to sit up and take notice. But, although I think I let her know more about me than many African children allow their parents, I became economical with the fullness of my runnings.

Romancing girls was one area I wanted to rap with her seriously about, but never got beyond relaying a few choice anecdotes. (She would be mildly amused and reiterate that, if I studied now, I could have all the time I wanted for girls later.) But they say that men look for the image of their mother in prospective partners, and I am increasingly aware of certain patterns in my tastes that I suspect are mother-related. Chubby cheeks, round faces and kind carers press those buttons, especially those receptive to whimsy.

Nor did she pay much mind to the substance of my youthful scribblings, which were profuse, except to take them to her office and return them for my perusal in the evening – typed out, pristine, and ready for whatever.

I was a smarmy seven or eight when I first gave her something to type. I had spotted a couple of mistakes in a book about Greek myths and wanted to send a letter to its publisher. She sorted it out for me and was as proud as my father when I got a letter back, thanking me and acknowledging the errors. That was the beginning of the Greeks and Romans phase of my life, and she typed untold lists and stories of gods, heroes and many-headed monsters. She always found the time. Later it was poetry and the thumping manuscript of a play. Her work on my behalf did not correspond to a larger endorsement of my ambition to write for a living. She would have been happy enough with me writing in my spare time, so long as I was a doctor, or failing that, a lawyer first.

Most likely, this was nothing more than an expression of the conviction held by most first-generation immigrants that the old professions were the safest places to reach for. Of course, I thought that my mother ought to treat me differently, and respect my wishes. I thought that that would be her instinct, if left to herself, and that when she continually pleaded with me to go down the medicine route I was hearing my father's voice. 'Mommy, don't tell me what he thinks. Tell me what you really think,' was my refrain.

The extent of her internal dialogue with these orthodoxies is a crucial part of that mystery which I will now struggle to unravel. I suspect that my notion of this freethinking unfettered ego, lurking beneath the lifelong layers of commitment and duties, was me juggling with the wrong ball again.

When she did express higher yearnings, they focused on returning home to Nigeria. I know she missed her family terribly, especially her own mother. She only saw most of them once after her departure in 1965 – when she returned for her father's funeral in the early '80's. I said that I would put her on a round-the-world cruise and she would smile, but it was home that she would speak and think of.

She would be so happy when Big Auntie, her older sister, came on holiday to stay with us. Big Auntie ran a clothes business and we were gratefully aware of her even before we met her, because big parcels would arrive from Lagos. The clothes tended to be of European design with little local glosses, and formed much of our casual wardrobe. But our debt to Auntie was owed, if anything, more to her ability to make us see our mother through new eyes. My folks were not people to have friends often in the house, and so it was a trip to see my mother doing her dailies animated by unconditional comradeship and shared history. I remember being struck by how brutal it must be to do without that dose of oxygen which most of us get from someone in our lives.

I met a friend of hers from work too, on the night of her fiftieth birthday dinner. I was intrigued at the prospect of seeing my mother anew again, and chatted with her friend at some length.

That was a truly special evening. My father took the whole family out to the Grosvenor House Hotel in the centre of town. It was the first time I had ever seen her being treated. She looked happy, elegant as ever, and so content with this little community that she had nurtured around her that I really began to believe in their masterplan. If those severities had to be endured so that this would be the way from now on – Mommy being spoilt, Mommy hanging out with her friends, the family together and in high spirits – then the whole coup was worth it. She seemed within sight of the payback on the gamble she had made when she forsook her home comforts.

The contrast between her home and away has become sharper for me because asthma, the disease which killed her, was a condition she developed in this country. And she only ever had it mildly, except on that fatal day. It has been difficult to resist casting her fate in a larger, symbolic, mould, and to read her life as a sacrifice in the struggle for her family to prosper.

That tendency is no doubt encouraged by the great weight that the mother-figure has carried in black popular culture. You'd be pushed to exaggerate the frequency with which the mother-image is invoked. Go to any Urban Poets' gig, and the 'Mother Africa/enduring rock, bearer of the burdens of the race' trope rivals that of Malcolm X for repetition and the reverence with which it is greeted. Check the literature from Toni Morrison's *Beloved* to Terry McMillan's *Mama*, to the vernacular which has given 'motherfucker' a particularly unbudgeable position in the dis ladder. No doubt the potency of the mother-figure across the diaspora is partly to do with the destruction wrought upon the integrity of the family by slavery and emigration. The fatherhood may be unclear, but you always know who the mother is.

Now that I approach my own long-awaited first visit to Nigeria, it seems clear to me that the trip's deeper purpose is all about my mother, African mothers, and me. About reclamation, and separating the romance and the myth from the real. I shall see Big Auntie again, and my mother's other siblings for the first time. I shall observe, trade anecdotes, and trace the kind of lines which will inevitably date this piece in my mind.

I still miss my mother terribly, and that absence will still be with me, but I hope to furnish my frequent voyages around her with new moorings and a future in all sorts of still secret places.

M e T o o

JAN DALLEY

Jan Dalley is the Literary Editor of the Independent
on Sunday. *She used to work in publishing. She lives
in London with her husband and three children.*

On the birth certificate of twins is marked the hour and
minute of their birth, as well as the date. Presumably this
official proof of seniority comes in handy for the rituals of
primogeniture – an inherited dukedom, say – but the majority
of twins have no need of such a document. They know only
too well whether they were born first or second, and they
rarely forget it. Other people know, too, if they are aware of
what to look for. Strange that an odd twenty minutes or so can
matter so much in a life, can define a psychology so powerfully.

I once amazed a man I met at a party (he was rather dull,
and therefore easy to amaze) by telling him after a quarter of
an hour's desultory chat that I knew he was a twin, and a second twin at that. Twin 2, as the doctors put it. He didn't
know whether to be pleased or not; on the whole, and understandably, he was annoyed at being spotted. But as far as I was
concerned he might as well have been holding up a placard,

because I was at the time so deeply involved with finding out about my own Twin 2.

L was born seventeen minutes after his sister S. She was moon-faced, determined at the breast, serene; he was squiggly, hungry, small, restless. In that witty-cruel way families have, A and I used to call him Me2: when the pair of them could hardly toddle, her mission was to find a patch of sunlight and sit in it, cooing and allowing others to pay her court, while he charged around after anyone and anything, lisping, 'Me too, me too, me too.' They were his first words. I doubt they will be his last, but on the way he will encounter a fair number of other adults (like that man at the party) who are also still yelling 'Me too', although they have learnt ways of doing it silently.

Twins are a marvel. Twins mean abundance and fecundity. Twins are also witchy, baffling, weird. In some tribal societies, twin-mothers were carried in procession to the fields to bless them and make them fertile; in others, they were shunned or even abandoned, thought to be tainted and possessed by evil forces. Our society, which often seems extremely primitive in its thinking about children, and does not much tell the truth about babies, turned out a fine display of both these attitudes.

I learnt that it is not allowed to complain about twins, or simply about having more babies than you wanted just at that particular moment. It is in very bad taste. Hollow laughter at the term 'family planning' is not acceptable. You are blessed by the gods, woman, so bloody well get on with it.

I wrote an article about the Multiple Birth Foundation for the *Observer*. It was purely objective, researched. The families on which that excellent organisation concentrate make my lot look like a picnic. These families all had triplets, quads and quins, often sick or disabled, sometimes already depleted by death and miscarriage. The babies were very often the unexpected result of fertility technologies, and a large number of the couples had split up under the strain. I pointed out that it was, in some cases, a bitter alternative to childlessness. The article was accompanied by a picture of me with my twins and their brother all sitting on my lap. I got hate mail, and perhaps I deserved it.

Mrs Headscarf stops me in the street, tears in her eyes as she gazes down at the buggy I have just exhaustedly shoved through yet another shop doorway that is too narrow. She stands – in my way – talking on and on: 'I *always* wanted twins.' It seems rude and cruel to say, 'Why?' And pointless. What I want to say is: 'I did not have "twins"; I just had two babies at once. Is that what you wanted?' Because I know perfectly well that what Mrs Headscarf thinks I have, and what she wants, is a Motherhood Badge with Bar sewn on to my Girl Guide uniform. I don't, I don't. Leave me alone.

After the babies were born, Angela Carter came to visit. She was writing, or thinking about writing, her wonderful book *Wise Children*, about a pair of theatrical sisters. I hardly knew her and it was a bit like being visited by the Queen. As if she'd come to declare us open, like a bridge or a power station. She brought her son's outgrown cot – a sweet and useful present, as we only had the one belonging to our first baby, and the twins were still sleeping in the baskets in which they were also lugged about, like bags of shopping, by day. With the cot she brought two blankets, for the new babies. Not particularly nice blankets, as a matter of fact: synthetic and already greyish from washing and inclined, later, to split, but I think I understood the gift for what it was – an offering. An offering to something we were both thinking about, I suppose, for she hardly glanced at the babies themselves. Sensible woman: she was fascinated by 'twins', but she knew they were just two babies.

When the twins were about two months old, we went to stay for the weekend with B and K. It was brave of them. They had a perfect family, we thought: a boy and a girl, both beautiful, the younger now reaching school age, freedom and clear water in sight ahead of them all. We had three babies under two (our eldest son was only one and a half when the twins were born); we'd arrived with nappies in industrial quantities, grey faces and very, very little to say to each other. B and K cheered us up, especially with a running joke that became more elaborate and preposterous as the weekend progressed, about how we were a walking contraceptive service – you only had to take one look at us and it was off to Marie Stopes for the snip, etc. We left a bit happier, counting the days until we were as free of babies as they already were. B and K's third child was born exactly nine months later.

It has been hard for A. He is the most organised and disciplined of people, and uses those possibly dreary-sounding attributes to great creative effect. What we now had was not what he wanted. He already knew about death, as something he could not control and could not reverse, but that birth should display the same characteristics was not something he had expected. He was not insensible to the richness of things, but it was as if he had been served a feast he hadn't ordered when he wasn't hungry. Friends were no help. A conversation about whether or not you can stand having the children you have is a dangerous one.

And what of Me2, the wriggling, fretful, 7lb instigator of all this emotional turmoil and hormonal chaos? Because there was little doubt in anyone's mind – even his own new-born psyche – that he was the extra one. We already had a dream-boat of a baby boy, and like many couples had thought we'd have another child because the first was so nice. Of course twins, even second twins, are not the only children who feel supernumerary, and this has nothing to do with numbers. But children are usually right in what they feel about themselves within a family, and if they are clever they can use it in the power-struggle of sibling relationships. So L, now nearly eight, has both the babyish insecurity of the am-I-wanted child, and the canny knowledge that he has the power to rock everybody's boat.

Scared of being overlooked, L chooses to be a stone in the shoe. Annoying, clumsy, clever, adorable, he has never had the security to make himself merely charming, simply easy. If only he knew. Far from being negligible, his impact has always been so strong that the difficulty is to concentrate on the other children. Even while his sister was being born, I could not keep my mind on her. The heart monitor strapped around me was registering *his* heartbeat, not hers; as I gave birth to one child the sound in my ears forced me to think of the other, because the familiar galloping-pony pulse had faltered terrifyingly down to a spluttering, agonised, pitifully irregular little drumbeat, sometimes stopping altogether as my heart stopped too, thinking he was dead as he struggled under the power of the contractions that gave her birth but only pummelled him in his uterine fastness.

Do this one quickly, or the other will die. Do this one right, or the other will be blind, deaf, dumb, brain-damaged. I wished I'd never read those statistics; but I had. The longer the first one takes, the more danger to the second. Do this one right and then do the other.

The night after L and S were born, I lay awake listening, trying to get used to the strange contents of the two cots crammed against my hospital bed. S was sleeping without a movement, almost without a sound, as effortlessly and efficiently as she had until that evening waited quietly, head-down on the launch-pad, for the moment of her birth. L lay in his cot, awake without crying, but never still. I watched his face that was never chubby and blurred like a baby's but already properly delineated and formed, like that of a miniature adult, a mannikin. He looked a bit tense, not with the vast and nameless terrors of infancy but with more adult concerns – as if he were facing an interview or a tricky committee meeting. His tiny feet twitched and worried the blanket, miniature hands with their long nails scrabbling at the covers, a moon-dancer out of his element crashed helplessly to earth. He seemed infinitely foreign – which was his planet? – but confusingly close. For a long moment I could not separate myself from him, or understand that he was outside me: I had felt the scrabbling fingers inside my belly, I had known that nervous twitching day and night for months as he swam and twisted high up under my ribcage, turning over and over.

It had been the usual antenatal hell, but very undramatic. Endless waiting; boring questions; proddings and mutterings; words like 'breech' and 'transverse'. I remember lying on my back pinned down by my belly, so immense and alien by then that it was as if a whale had somehow slithered in under my skin and taken up residence. 'Twin 1, no problem,' the consultant said over his shoulder to his group of students. 'All in order. But she'll have trouble with this second one. Lying all wrong. Head's there' – jab under my right armpit – 'and feet somewhere around here' – jab at my left side, roughly where my waist must have been, a hundred years earlier. 'No chance.' He turned to me – that is, my face, my thinking self – for the first time since he'd walked in. 'Caesar, I think, Mrs Umer . . . best thing, really.' And he swept out of the cubicle with his students fluttering after him like a pack of chickens.

Caesar yerself, fatso. Consultants treat you like a dumb child, and make you childish. For the first of many times since, I consulted the bustling little entity that later became L and we made our pact against the world, not mother and infant now but two naughty children cooking up a prank to annoy Sir. Fear of knife. Worse than maths homework. Be a pal and sort it out for me? And when the time came, he did. Although he seemed better placed to be born through my mouth than by any more conventional route, and although we were both by then more inclined just to go to sleep and forget it till the morning, he performed a sudden, giant, fishy flip and dived head first like a nervous swimmer off a high board. Rushing out, ungainly, busy, eager, unexpected. Me too.

Fatso was on the golf course at the time, the nurses told me, and instead there was a nice enough man to whom I talked – so A told me later – vivaciously and incoherently about horses. The connection was perfectly logical to me at the time. He was wearing white wellingtons splattered with what could well have been blood and the whole business had made me think of abattoirs, of my pony that went barmy and went to the knackers and the difficulty in feeding the dog, after that, in case it was him in the tin. The pony, that is. Anyway, when Mr Big made his royal progress the next day I could tell he was annoyed. 'Sometimes they turn . . . .' The students dutifully looked annoyed, too. I looked at the mannikin. He was back on his own planet, for the time being, but there was a hint of satisfaction in his bleary gaze. We'd done it, he and I.

So it began well. I still have the sense that he and I are together against the world, but mostly because I feel I must protect him. Partly against anyone who thinks he is extra, or marvellous. But mostly against the day-to-day. He is not easy to have as a child, or as a brother. He is impish and talented and will not let us relax. He has a lot of accidents, always to his right side, often to his face, which already has two quite bad scars, and invariably at moments of stress. He always has a new best friend. He will be successful, in my fantasies: he will crash a lot of cars, be loved by lots of girls and cost us a lot of money. He will not quite do what he should, for the devil in him, or for simple curiosity. I will have to bail him out, of something, some time. I cannot imagine loving him more, but I do not love him better than my other children. That problem at least has never posed itself. And, for all my protectiveness, I also know that, of all my children, he may be the one who needs me least.

The years of baby-hell are over, the house ruthlessly cleared of every last bib and rattle and fetching red gumboot. There is none of that sort of nostalgia around here. Angela Carter's cot long ago collapsed, or went off to a deserving home; I can't remember which. The only things that linger in the back of a cupboard somewhere are two much ripped and sucked off-white baby blankets. I think I will keep those; goodness knows why.

SPIKE MILLIGAN

Spike Milligan was born in 1918. Actor, humanist, composer, painter, poet and conservationist, he is the author of over forty books and was co-founder of the Goon Show.

My Mother

So my mother, my mother
    laid to rest
The fairy dances fade
    but cannot end
The dolls stand
    serious faced
In your empty room
    cast glass eyes
At the Burmese lacquer
I left the piano lid open
So you can play for dad
The love lyrics
    The Cubanola Glide
The Officers' mess glasses

from Belgaum
Have drunk their last
regimental toast
You left the house full
of everything
Mostly love.
Goodbye for a while mum.
Remember Rangoon mum
the concerts and the Brigade dance
you made your own dress
White organdie.

And Poona.
You must have loved Poona
The Governor's Ball
– you singing with the band.
How wonderful it must have been
Heidsieck's Monopole!
all your life.
I can't say how much
I love you.
The language wasn't invented
I rang Woy Woy 413662 today
You didn't answer
You must have been out.

The Disqualified Horse

___

VICTORIA GLENDINNING

Victoria Glendinning is a biographer, novelist and journalist.

___

There's no love without pain. That's the grossly simple lesson of this book. Talking to our fellow-contributors and reading what they have written, we've been struck by their courage and generosity in putting themselves through what has in some cases turned out to be an ordeal. There has been intense pleasure in it too.

For Matthew and me, it has been a weird experience. Like you, reading this book now, we have entered into the relationships of other mothers and sons – learning only one side of each story. At the same time we were investigating our own, from both points of view. We have laughed a lot, and argued a lot, and wept a bit (me, anyway), and learnt to be merciful. It has been incredibly worthwhile.

Mothers and daughters can seemingly rabbit on endlessly about one another without difficulty, however fraught the relationship. Mothers and sons, when they look below the surface, find unconditional love – and below that again a tangle of passion, resentment, longing, ambivalence, incomprehension and taboo. I wrote to a friend asking her to write about her son for this book. She replied with regret that she just couldn't – or, 'not yet'. She said that 'it – or rather he – is so close and the whole business so present that I can't understand any of it, I'm afraid'.

Her son is a student; all mine are well past that stage. But I recognise what she is saying; and what she maybe doesn't know yet is that it's never over. It remains always 'present', and always difficult to understand.

Weeks ago, when I was beginning this piece, I rang Matthew to ask about something factual that I couldn't remember. He was starting his piece too. This was a very peculiar situation, each of us sitting in front of a word-processor writing about our experience of the other.

It wasn't a very long conversation because he was 'a bit sore with me', as he said. This has happened rather a lot. He is a very open person and talks to me a great deal about himself, about how his work is going, about his personal life, about how he is feeling. And if he is angry about something I have said, he lets me know.

I'm by no means the only person he talks to, and I don't believe I'm the only person whom he gets sore with, either. But because we are in constant communication, and very close geographically as well as in other ways, and because I'm his Mum, I guess I have had the undiluted essence of it.

His soreness with me has generally been caused by my

responding to something he tells me in a way that seems to him unfair or unsupportive; or by my seeming to make assumptions that he finds unacceptable; or by my asking something of him that seems to him unreasonable.

Sometimes the rift has been caused by a misunderstanding, and is put right immediately. Sometimes it takes several days. I haven't always felt that I have been in the wrong, even though I accept his perception that I am. Sometimes I think that I am definitely in the wrong. It's best if I don't comment too much on what he tells me, unless specifically asked to. I can be too quick and definite in my responses, and can sound combative or dismissive. Matthew is not the only person who has complained about this. But I guess he has inherited the trait, because he is always sure what he thinks about people and situations. His brothers are pretty uncompromising too.

Anyway, Matthew and I have had this ritual of an offence unintentionally committed (by me), followed by analysis of the offence (from him), followed by defence or apology or both (from me), followed by a period of coolness (from him), followed by his announcing that it's all right again, followed by a return to calm, happy waters.

And almost at once, on that particular occasion, he rang me back. We were OK again.

A lot has happened between us since we started putting this book together and writing our own bits. We have talked so much. I have learnt a great deal, and feel as if a lot of dirt had been cleared away from under the fingernails of my soul. If I have a soul, which I doubt. So it might as well have fingernails.

The occasional tensions between us, however, have made for an exhilarating kind of dynamic – though if that sort of stuff were all there was to our relationship, I probably wouldn't be writing about him, and we certainly wouldn't be able to work on *Sons and Mothers* together.

Matthew and I always make each other laugh a lot. He is very quick-minded and clever and original. He can be brilliantly funny. His stepfather, Terence, who loved all four boys and saw their special qualities, said Matthew was the one who knew how to make him laugh.

That's not all, either. The very personal conversations have never been just one-way. It's not just him telling me things. I tell Matthew private things too, I guess more than I tell anyone else. Unless he has too much on his mind – and I wouldn't start in, if I saw that was the case – he always listens carefully, understands what I am saying, makes measured and enlightening comments, gives himself entirely to the problem, and doesn't try and hurry me on to something else.

Once, recently, he had already got up to leave when I said something about troubles. 'Troubles? What troubles?' And he sat down again at the kitchen table, as if he had all the time in the world. Most so-called sensitive people are sensitive only about themselves. He is sensitive to others too, and sharply aware of the emotional climate in any gathering. I think he brokers quite a lot of what goes on between the rest of us, without our always knowing it.

His sensitivity has taken a bashing. After he had finished his degree at Sussex University, he had a depression. Nigel (the boys' father) and I had been in the process of splitting up over four years, from when he was thirteen. The connection between these two events cannot be proved, but obviously there is one.

While this was going on, he lived a lot with Nigel. I was never out of contact with him, but it was a horrible time. I don't know whether it would have been better or worse, for him, if we had had family therapy. It might have been better for me. His shrink belonged to the school that entertains no communication with other members of the family, so the rest of us did not know how to help, or in what ways we were making things better or worse. I have never felt so useless, or so unhappy. This is an egotistic thing to say, because what he was going through was obviously much worse.

When he was at Sussex, and enjoying his life there, I used to drive him down to Brighton sometimes at the beginning of term. I liked those drives. We talked, and had fry-ups at the Happy Eater. I apologised to him in the car one time for what I felt was a particularly bad incident during the break-up with his father. No, said Matthew, it was not that he minded so much. It was that I had not talked to him enough about what was happening. I left most of it to Dad.

Why did I not talk more openly to Matthew, or to his brothers, about what was happening? I know they all suffered because of this, and have had to come to terms with the break-up over time and in their own ways. We have talked about it since, as I could not then.

My feeling at the time was that I was protecting them from unnecessary knowledge and unnecessary suffering. I think now that my guilt towards them was so huge, and my infidelity to them so painful, that I just couldn't face them with it. I wanted their lives to continue unscathed, which of course was impossible.

When Matthew was depressed, he did a lot of drawing and painting. Afterwards, he did a year at art school. He gave me a picture he had done called *The Disqualified Horse*. It had won its race, but then been disqualified for some misdemeanour. In Matthew's picture, based on a newspaper photograph, the disqualified horse, with the dejected jockey on its back, is being led in by four men. The disqualified horse was me. It's a pretty good picture; I still have it.

Matthew still draws and paints; he writes a lot of poems too, about all kinds of things and about his girlfriend. Writing is his work now. He writes, mostly about sport, for newspapers and magazines. He does radio work too. It gives me a very strange feeling, hearing his voice coming out of the radio. He is very good at all he does. I am often astonished and humbled by the quality of what he writes.

Because of Matthew's period of depression in his early twenties, I remain peculiarly vulnerable to his troubles, as he is to mine. But as soon as I write this sentence, I want to put in a non-exclusivity clause, for I would also describe myself as peculiarly vulnerable to each of the other sons' troubles. I also feel fiercely proud – not proud *of* them, but proud *for* them and all they do and are. It's a savagely loving business.

If I am anything to go by, all mothers are in love with their sons. But because I am daughterless, I love their girlfriends too, as I love my stepdaughters. I love the boys' girlfriends because it is easy – they are exceptional – but even if it were difficult I should love them. It was sometimes quite lonely, when the boys were young, being the only female in a household of males. There is an otherness that is fascinating, but unbridgeable. I remember the moment when it seemed right that the elder ones should be told the facts of life. I thought it more suitable that their father should do this, and he duly went upstairs to talk to them when they were in bed. A little later, I heard roars of laughter coming from upstairs. I felt mystified, and excluded. A bit *offended*.

But Paul, the eldest, doesn't remember that at all. He remembers me taking him into the bathroom – the only place in the house where we could be alone – telling him the facts of life, and making him promise not to tell the others. Well, I don't remember that at all. It's like that with Matthew – as you will notice, even when we remember the same things, we remember them a bit differently.

It's quite rare for me now to be with all four sons together. But I like it, when it happens. Each of them, separately, means something to me that no one else ever can. To see them all together in a room spells for me total security and – what? – repose, appeasement. I really admire parents of single children. The only thing that has prevented me devouring my progeny with my love is the fact that there are four of them. The load is shared – mercifully, for me and, even more, for them.

The boys always formed a strong unit, with close alliances between any two of them shifting at different stages in their growing up. Matthew's brothers, as well as the rest of our widely extended family, are part of his story. They are part of mine too.

We are a demonstrative family. The men hug and kiss one another as freely as the women. I am of a cheerful, optimistic disposition and presume everything is 'all right' unless something bad happens. This may have put pressure on the children to be 'all right' too, when they weren't. When I am not all right, they are good at putting me together again, and I try to do the same for them. But it's hard sometimes to know whether you are being intrusive, and whether someone wants to talk or not.

We are all good at having a good time. The good times are genuine. What's the point of *not* having fun? Terence used to say that I lacked the tragic sense of life, and though he said it in a joking way he made it sound like a reproach. But I think it is morally better to be contented when you can. The downside is, that in this default-mode of contentedness, the negative passions, and tensions, betrayals and disappointments, tend to be submerged, surfacing only in times of crisis. As time goes by, maybe because we all live different and separate lives now, it seems easier to talk about problems and difficulties, and less threatening.

I have more than one son, but each of them only has one mother. For him, there is no sharing of that particular load. Once, when Matthew was little and we were living in Ireland, I picked up a rock that I liked, and he carried it all the way up a mountain for me. He said, in a dark time, that he felt he was always carrying a heavy rock up a mountain for me. I did not ask him to carry either the real rock or the metaphorical one. But I let him.

I still have that rock, it has moved everywhere with me and is now in the pond outside this house.

Matthew is the third of the four brothers, all very close to one another in age. My mother used to say that a third child had particular difficulties and particular characteristics. She was a third child, and she was talking about herself, not Matthew. In any case, I guess that Paul would have something to say about the special pressures of being the eldest; Hugo might feel he had once had to fight for his identity as the second son; and Simon, as a vociferous toddler, made it clear that there was a very special battle to be fought as the youngest of four.

All the clichés are true. Childhood is so short. Where has the time gone? How did that become this? When I look at pictures of Matthew and his brothers as children – knowing so well their little bodies and the texture of their hair, their attitudes and expressions, all their toys and T-shirts and bicycles, and the garden in Spain, the garden in Southampton, the garden in Dublin – it seems that I could merge into the photographs and take our life up again at any point; that I could run in my bikini under the Spanish sun and pick little Matthew up from where he is wandering away on his own down the beach at Ampurias, and carry him, squalling, back to the picnic and the towels. I can't. That sweet life with the children is over for ever.

The mother's tragedy is that her sons never knew her when she was young, though it is then that she is closest to them, physically. They knew, then, her smell and her skin and her touch. And her clothes: Hugo asked me not long ago if I had ever had a fluffy brown sweater, because he had a memory of being held against it when he was very small. I did have a brown angora sweater, though I had forgotten it until he resurrected his own early memory. But they don't remember, really, how I was in my mid-twenties. Sons see their mothers 'now', so their most lasting memory will be of a leathery old crone (unless I go under a bus rather soon).

This regret is not based merely on vanity. There is something more profound, to do with the way my memories differ from theirs. When I think about Matthew, I can see every phase of his life at once, from babyhood on, surreally juxtaposed and in no particular order.

Matthew was an irresistible pretty child, with straight fair hair, big blue eyes, a wide smile. Handsomeness has been one of his assets. Has he sometimes leant too heavily on its effect? Like his brothers he is effortlessly good at games. This stood them in good stead when they were moved from a small, liberal school in Ireland, perched on the top of a hill over the sea, straight into a fairly rough London comprehensive.

Matthew coped as well as anyone. He has always adored football and playing football. He still plays football. He is extremely sociable when he feels like it and has a formidable charm which grows out of kindness and interest. But he has always needed a lot of time to himself. Nowadays, if I ask him round when I have visitors, he will initially say 'No'. But then, he will usually change his mind and come. And I am pleased, and so are the visitors.

When he was little, he had a collection of Dinky and Matchbox cars. Quite often, he played elaborate, secret, silent games with them for hours alone up in his room. I worried about this quite a bit. I see now I was jealous of the cars, too. I threw them out, without asking him. He was almost grown up then and hadn't looked at them for years. But still, I shouldn't have done it. At the time, I didn't try and put a stop to it because I thought, in such a large and noisy family, it was an important way of making his own space.

I did sometimes go up to his room and try to persuade him to come down if he was playing with the cars when visitors came, because I did not want him to exclude himself from sociable events. Also, I wanted to teach him hospitable manners. He always resisted. Sitting back on his haunches on the coffee-coloured carpet, moving the cars around according to some mysterious ritual, he went on playing.

I asked him about this, long after. He said: 'Why did you only tell me to come downstairs when there were visitors? Why didn't you ask me to come down just to be with you?'

Why didn't I? Because I didn't want to violate his need for privacy. Because I didn't know that 'being with me' would have been any lure at all. I thought, rather, that he used these withdrawals to get away from me, and everyone else, for a bit. I thought that was what he wanted and needed. I got it wrong.

One of the hardest things for me as a mother was the cruel crashing of gears as the boys grew up. When they are young, it is your duty to know what they are doing every minute of the day. The boys were my single biggest preoccupation, and their lives consumed most of my energy and my own life. I didn't resent this. I had a difficult childhood myself. I re-wrote it, in happiness, through my children's childhood.

They were brought up with a lot of freedom and very few rules. (Though I do hear the echo of my voice shouting for the hundredth time, as loud crashes came from the sitting-room, 'Don't play football in the house!') If I had my time over, I would teach them more of the world's rules. But I guess I was too indulgent to discipline either myself or them, and anyway I was around all of the time when they were little, so could prevent them from harming themselves, most of the time.

Then, as they got older, all the strong emotional muscles which over the years made me automatically and efficiently watchful, responsive and physically intimate with them, ceased to be needed. It was more extreme than just not being needed. If I went on responding as before, I would be harming them. What had once been essential would now be over-protective, possessive, intrusive. So everything had to be thrown into reverse.

I found this process so painful that when Simon, the youngest, left home, and for the first time there was no 'child' in the house, I had to write myself a stern memo – I was on a train, I remember, and wrote it with tears trickling down my face – to the effect that I had no rights in them, they were only lent to me, and that if I expected them all to ring me up virtually on a daily basis I was a monster and a fool.

What I have learnt since is that when boys leave home a new relationship has to be tacitly negotiated with each. And it is negotiated *on his terms*. That's the point. Some want more contact than others. Some are more naturally communicative. This has absolutely no bearing on who loves whom most. It is no good the mother saying, this is how I want it to be. If you let the relationship settle down *on his terms*, then both parties will be content.

All of them except Simon went abroad for most of their 'gap year' before they left for university. Paul went to work in France. (He learnt about his parents' separation by post. Oh hell.) Matthew followed Hugo in going to Israel to work on a kibbutz. Unlike Hugo, Matthew didn't have friends to stay with when he first arrived, and I felt anxious. I wrote a sort of love-letter which I slipped into his travelling-bag, so that he would find it on arrival. (I should like to write him a love-letter now. Perhaps this is one.) Matthew got bad tonsillitis when he was in Israel, and wrote to us from a hospital in Tel Aviv. This was terrifying – and my feeling for him became inflamed into agitated anxiety.

Separation anxieties, for me, started much earlier. I married at the end of my second year at university, had my first child within a year, and so had no adult life as just myself. I came to see myself not *as* myself, but as the mother of four little boys. When one by one they started school, and I no longer went everywhere surrounded by a quartet of small heads in shades from brown to blond, Matthew's the blondest of them all, I felt worthless, and invisible.

Yet I was trying to write before Matthew even started at school. I shut myself in the back bedroom at Southampton on Tuesday afternoons when Mrs Bailey came to clean. Mrs Bailey was fat and warm and she and Matthew got on well. I know it was Mrs Bailey, and not an au pair girl (as I see Matthew says in his introduction), because if there had been an au pair girl the back bedroom would have been hers, and I could not have worked in there. Anyway, I could hear her outside the door telling Matthew not to go into that room because Mummy was working, and Mummy would be cross if she was disturbed.

But the door handle turned, the door slowly opened wide, and there stood Matthew – smiling hopefully, just demonstrating his presence, just testing. I should have pretended to be cross, if only to back up Mrs Bailey and to teach Matthew something about limits and boundaries. But I couldn't help being pleased to see him. 'Hello, Matthew!'

I still say 'Hello, Matthew!' often. I see and talk to all these men who are, who were, my children with comfortable frequency. But at the moment, I see Matthew more often than I see any of his brothers. This is because of geography, and pure chance. His flat is about a hundred yards from my house. The flat is part of a house that Terence and I lived in formerly; we sold the rest of it when we moved across the road and down the lane.

I have another and quite different life in Ireland, but it's in London that Matthew's life and mine run in parallel. Matthew works from home, and so do I. We both live alone. We do the same kind of work. He comes over to use my fax, or to take a coffee break, or to show me something he is writing, or to tell me about a telephone conversation with Pippa, or for no reason at all; he doesn't need a reason. Sometimes we make a definite arrangement and go out to lunch or dinner in a restaurant, in order to have a different kind of conversation than the ongoing, on-flowing one at my kitchen table. I liked going in to the Academy Club in Soho when he used to work there, and the big blond man behind the bar said, 'Hello, Mum' – with a quick look to see who I was with.

Since Terence died in June 1994, Matthew's nearness has been a lifeline. He is such a good friend to me. Perhaps the continuing proximity is not pure chance. We both know it is not for ever. It is just for now. But just for now, it is wonderful. Most people avoid the grief of others, and assume that with the passing of the months recovery has taken place. Matthew will ask me what I am thinking and feeling now about the loss of Terence, and about the way my new life is going.

Matthew is not afraid of grief, which means that he is not afraid of anything.

I want to rewind the film and go back to the beginning. Matthew was born on 25 September. It was a home birth. A few weeks earlier we had moved from Oxford to Southampton, where as yet we knew no one.

We always seemed to be in transit when we had a baby. I had gone into hospital to have my second son, Hugo, the very night of our previous move, eighteen months earlier. This curious timing began to worry my mother – even though it was she who insisted we come up to London when Paul, the eldest, was imminent, because she wanted him to be born in Westminster Hospital, where she did voluntary work with the Red Cross, taking the book-trolley round the wards. I was very young then. Now I had moved out of her control. 'Your womb will fall out on the pavement,' she said darkly, when we moved house yet again a week after Matthew's younger brother, Simon, was born, also at home.

That first house in Southampton was rented – an unmodernised, detached, red-brick Victorian villa with a neglected back garden full of long grass and old apple trees. My diary for 25 September reads as follows:

> Gas man [in ink]
> Boys Hair 10. [in red crayon]

Carpet delivered [in pencil]
Matthew born 8.20 am [in ink]
G's come [in ink]

The G's are Nigel's parents. I hope the gas man and the carpet arrived, but I can't remember. I don't know if the boys got
their haircuts. My mother visited the next day. I see that the
carpet-layer was booked in for the next day as well. I expect
he came too.

We were given a long list of necessary equipment by the
midwife which included clean, empty fish-paste pots. We
didn't eat fish-paste and had to buy some specially. I could not
think what purpose they might serve. In the event, they were
just for standing thermometers and clean spoons in.

Having the baby at home was much better for me than the
two hospital births had been. The doctor missed the moment,
but came afterwards to put in some stitches. I liked being in
my own bed, all crunchy with the newspapers that the midwife spread under the sheet. Nigel was there all the time.

When Matthew arrived, his elder brothers – Paul, aged
three, Hugo, eighteen months – were having their cornflakes
downstairs. When everything had been tidied up they came
up with Sharon and we said, 'What is there in this room that
was not here yesterday?' Paul and Hugo gazed around blankly
for quite a long time before spotting the Moses basket on its
stand, and Matthew in it.

Sharon was the mother's help whom we had taken on to
see us over the move and the birth. Sharon thought very little of us. When we bought some bit of furniture from a junk
shop she looked at it scornfully and said, 'It's not very *modern*,

is it?' She made the same complaint about the house, and she was right. It had no heating. Matthew was the smallest of the babies, only 5$^1/_2$ lb at birth, so he had to be fed at frequent intervals. It was a chilly autumn. We lit a fire in the bedroom grate at night, and I would sit beside it to feed Matthew in the small hours, liking it.

Matthew may have been small at birth, but he caught up quickly. He is a big man, six feet three inches tall. He was very healthy as a baby, with a strong hold on life, and he ate everything that he could lay his mouth and hands on. I see him in his high chair, cramming food into his face, squashing some of it with the flat of his hands on the tray of the chair, opening his fists to splat dollops of it on to the black-and-white kitchen lino. I can hear Dominique, the French au pair girl who succeeded Sharon, saying in despair: 'Matthieu, tu es dégolace! [You are disgusting!]' All little children do this when they are learning to feed themselves, but Matthew did it with spectacular virtuosity and pleasure.

He has always been healthy, apart from the bout of tonsillitis in Israel. About a year ago, he had bad tonsillitis again. He had a high fever, his throat closed up, he could hardly breathe, his face was grey. He was, suddenly, very ill.

While I sat with him in the Royal Free, waiting for a doctor to see him, and then for a bed to become available, he was stoical. He didn't have the strength to be anything else. Beside him, I was consumed by the ancient agonies of any mother whose child is perhaps in danger. But he is a grown man.

That singleminded, obsessive savagery of mother-love is muffled in me now, except when one of them is ill or troubled. They remain my first concern and I would die to save any of them. But I have become individual and single, and so busy that even Sophie, the dog, gets shorter shrift than she should. When I am away, I may not consciously think of Matthew at all for a while. But I know that my conversation with him, in one form or another, will last as long as my life.

And I realise that my sons being there, living their separate crowded adult lives, yet still and always embedded in me, is what gives meaning to my existence. I don't imagine that this is the case for them, in reverse. That doesn't matter.

Matthew – thank you for doing this book with me.